D0495470

The Australian Women's Weekly cookbooks

Chicken seems to have been designed for the way we like to cook in this new millennium, and its immense popularity can be attributed to both how easy it is to prepare and how quickly it transforms itself into a meal – every recipe in this book makes it to the table in half an hour or less. One of my favourite tricks is to buy a barbecued chicken on my way home, then use the meat as the main ingredient in a pasta sauce, soup, stir-fry or salad... talk about Meals in Minutes!

Pamela Clark

Food Director

contents

in a wok	4
in the oven	36
on the grill	52
take one barbecued chicken...	74
chicken cuts	114
glossary	116
index	118
facts and figures	119

in a wok

chicken, pide and haloumi salad

Assemble this salad just before serving.

300g prepared mixed vegetable antipasto
500g tenderloins, chopped coarsely
2 tablespoons pine nuts
1/2 long loaf pide
250g haloumi cheese
200g baby rocket leaves
170g marinated artichoke hearts, drained, quartered
250g cherry tomatoes
1/4 cup (60ml) balsamic vinegar

1 Drain antipasto in strainer over small bowl; reserve 1/3 cup of the oil. Chop antipasto finely.

2 Heat 1 tablespoon of the reserved oil in wok or large frying pan; stir-fry chicken, in batches, until browned all over and cooked through. Cover to keep warm. Stir-fry pine nuts in same wok until lightly browned.

3 Cut pide into 1cm slices; grill until browned both sides. Cut haloumi crossways into 16 slices. Heat 1 tablespoon of the reserved oil in same wok; cook haloumi, in batches, until browned both sides.

4 Toss antipasto, chicken, pide and haloumi in large bowl with rocket, artichoke and tomatoes. Drizzle with combined remaining oil and vinegar; sprinkle with pine nuts.

SERVES 4

per serving 47.8g fat; 3335kJ

tips Haloumi is a firm salty cheese, available from most delicatessens and some supermarkets.

If there is not enough oil in the mixed vegetable antipasto to make 1/3 cup, add olive oil to make up the required amount.

chicken and couscous salad

PREPARATION TIME 10 MINUTES • COOKING TIME 10 MINUTES

Couscous, made from durum wheat semolina, is originally from North Africa and is available at most supermarkets. You can use whatever flavour pesto you prefer as a substitute for the sun-dried tomato variety.

1 tablespoon olive oil
800g tenderloins,
   chopped coarsely
$^2/_3$ cup (160ml) chicken stock
20g butter
$^2/_3$ cup (130g) couscous
2 teaspoons finely grated
   lemon rind
$^1/_3$ cup (90g) sun-dried
   tomato pesto
2 tablespoons lemon juice
250g baby rocket leaves

1 Heat oil in wok or large frying pan; stir-fry chicken, in batches, until browned all over and cooked through.

2 Meanwhile, bring stock to a boil in medium saucepan; stir in butter, couscous and rind. Remove from heat. Cover; stand about 5 minutes or until water is absorbed, fluffing couscous with fork occasionally.

3 Whisk pesto and juice in large bowl. Add couscous, chicken and rocket; toss gently to combine.

SERVES 4

per serving 29.4g fat; 2425kJ

tip Chicken strips or chicken stroganoff are available at many butchers or poultry shops and can be substituted for the chicken tenderloins, if desired.

chicken and almonds

PREPARATION TIME 15 MINUTES • COOKING TIME 15 MINUTES

**1 cup (160g) blanched
whole almonds**
1 tablespoon peanut oil
**750g breast fillets,
sliced thinly**
**1 medium red onion (170g),
chopped coarsely**
**1 small leek (200g),
sliced thickly**
2 cloves garlic, crushed
2 tablespoons hoisin sauce
**200g green beans,
trimmed, halved**
**2 trimmed sticks celery (150g),
sliced thinly**
1 tablespoon light soy sauce
1 tablespoon plum sauce

1 Heat wok or large frying pan.
Stir-fry almonds until lightly
browned; remove from wok.
Heat half of the oil in same
wok; stir-fry chicken, in batches,
until browned all over and
cooked through.

2 Heat remaining oil in wok;
stir-fry onion, leek and garlic
until fragrant. Add hoisin sauce,
beans and celery; stir-fry until
beans are just tender. Return
chicken to wok with remaining
sauces; stir-fry until heated
through. Toss almonds through
chicken mixture.

SERVES 4

per serving 38g fat; 2524kJ

tip You can use cashews instead
of almonds, if preferred.

serving suggestion Serve with
a bowl of steamed jasmine rice.

cantonese stir-fry on noodle cakes

PREPARATION TIME 10 MINUTES • COOKING TIME 20 MINUTES

You need a piece of fresh ginger measuring about 1cm in length for this recipe.

**2 x 85g packets chicken flavour
  2-minute noodles**
1 tablespoon peanut oil
500g breast fillets, sliced thinly
**1 medium red onion (100g),
  sliced thickly**
2 cloves garlic, crushed
10g fresh ginger, sliced thinly
**1 medium carrot (120g),
  sliced thinly**
**1 large red capsicum (350g),
  sliced thinly**
1 tablespoon cornflour
3/4 cup (180ml) chicken stock
500g baby bok choy, quartered
1/3 cup (80ml) black bean sauce

1 Place noodles in medium heatproof bowl; cover with boiling water. Stand until just tender; drain. Toss one flavour sachet gently through noodles (reserve remaining sachet for another use).

2 Heat half of the oil in medium frying pan. Add a quarter of the noodles. Using metal spatula or wooden spoon to form into "cake" shape; press down on cake firmly. Cook until browned both sides; repeat with remaining noodles to make four noodle cakes in total.

3 Meanwhile, heat remaining oil in wok or large frying pan; stir-fry chicken, in batches, until cooked through. Place onion, garlic and ginger; stir-fry until onion just softens. Add carrot and capsicum; stir-fry until vegetables are just tender.

4 Blend cornflour with stock in small jug. Return chicken to wok with bok choy, cornflour mixture and sauce; stir-fry until bok choy just wilts and sauce thickens slightly. Serve noodle cakes topped with chicken stir-fry.

SERVES 4

per serving 20.7g fat; 1988kJ

tips This recipe is best made close to serving time.

To reduce cooking time, toss the drained noodles with chicken stir-fry instead of making noodle cakes.

serving suggestion Spring rolls would make a great appetiser before serving this recipe.

Toss one flavour sachet through the drained noodles

Press cooked noodles firmly to form a "cake" shape

chicken and mixed mushroom stir-fry

PREPARATION TIME 15 MINUTES • COOKING TIME 10 MINUTES

600g hokkien noodles
1 tablespoon peanut oil
750g tenderloins, halved
200g button mushrooms, halved
200g flat mushrooms,
**   sliced thickly**
200g swiss brown
**   mushrooms, halved**
3 green onions,
**   chopped finely**
2 tablespoons mild chilli sauce
1/2 cup (125ml) oyster sauce

1 Rinse noodles in strainer under hot water. Separate noodles with fork; drain.

2 Heat half of the oil in wok or large frying pan; stir-fry chicken, in batches, until browned all over and cooked through.

3 Heat remaining oil in wok; stir-fry mushrooms, in batches, until browned. Return chicken and mushrooms to wok with noodles, onion and sauces; stir-fry until heated through.

SERVES 4

per serving 16.5g fat; 2342kJ

tip Also known as cremini or roman mushrooms, swiss browns have a strong, earthy flavour.

serving suggestion Steamed gow gees, purchased from your local Asian supermarket, make a tasty starter to this stir-fry.

wok-tossed honey soy wings

PREPARATION TIME 10 MINUTES • COOKING TIME 15 MINUTES

12 large wings (1.5kg)
3 cloves garlic, crushed
1 tablespoon grated fresh ginger
1 tablespoon peanut oil
1 tablespoon fish sauce
1 tablespoon light soy sauce
¼ cup (90g) honey
2 green onions, sliced thinly

1 Cut wing tips from chicken; cut wings in half at joint.

2 Combine chicken in large bowl with garlic and ginger. Heat oil in wok or large frying pan; stir-fry chicken mixture, in batches, until chicken is lightly browned.

3 Return chicken mixture to wok. Add sauces and honey; stir-fry until well coated. Cover wok; cook, stirring occasionally, about 10 minutes or until chicken is cooked through. Top with onion.

SERVES 4

per serving 17.2g fat; 1881kJ

tip This recipe is best made close to serving time.

serving suggestion Serve with steamed jasmine rice and stir-fried bok choy.

Cut wing tips from pieces

Cut wings in half at joint

nuggets with roast kumara and rocket

PREPARATION TIME 10 MINUTES • COOKING TIME 20 MINUTES

1 large kumara (500g), peeled
cooking-oil spray
1 small brown onion (80g),
    chopped finely
700g mince
1/2 cup loosely packed, coarsely
    chopped fresh flat-leaf parsley
1 egg
1¹/2 cups (100g) stale
    breadcrumbs
1/2 cup (50g) packaged
    breadcrumbs
1 tablespoon olive oil
100g rocket

DIPPING SAUCE
1/3 cup (80ml) tomato sauce
2 tablespoons barbecue sauce
1 tablespoon sugar
1 tablespoon malt vinegar

1 Preheat oven to moderately hot.

2 Cut kumara lengthways into thin slices; cut slices lengthways into chip-sized pieces. Place kumara, in single layer, on oiled oven tray; coat with cooking-oil spray. Roast, uncovered, about 20 minutes or until browned and just tender.

3 Combine onion, chicken, parsley, egg and stale breadcrumbs in medium bowl; using hand, mix well. Shape tablespoons of chicken mixture into nuggets; roll nuggets in packaged breadcrumbs.

4 Heat half of the oil in wok or large frying pan; stir-fry half of the nuggets until browned all over and cooked through. Repeat with remaining oil and nuggets.

5 Serve nuggets with rocket, kumara and separate bowl of dipping sauce.

dipping sauce Combine ingredients in small bowl.

MAKES 24

per serving 22.6g fat; 2527kJ

Cut kumara lengthways into thin slices

Cut kumara slices into chips

Roll nuggets in packaged breadcrumbs

chicken satay

PREPARATION TIME 5 MINUTES • COOKING TIME 10 MINUTES

The spiciness of this dish will depend on which brand of satay sauce you use.

1 tablespoon peanut oil
750g tenderloins, halved
2 large brown onions (400g), sliced thickly
1 clove garlic, crushed
1/4 cup (60ml) chicken stock
2/3 cup (160ml) coconut milk
3/4 cup (180ml) satay sauce

1 Heat oil in wok or large frying pan; stir-fry chicken, in batches, until browned all over and cooked through.

2 Place onion and garlic in same wok; stir-fry until onion softens. Return chicken to wok with remaining ingredients; stir-fry until sauce thickens slightly.

SERVES 4

per serving 34g fat; 2353kJ

tip Add some whole roasted peanuts for extra crunch.

serving suggestion Accompany satay with steamed long-grain white rice and top with thinly sliced green onion.

lemon grass and asparagus chicken

PREPARATION TIME 15 MINUTES • COOKING TIME 15 MINUTES

**500g breast fillets,
sliced thickly**
3 cloves garlic, crushed
**2 tablespoons finely chopped
fresh lemon grass**
1 teaspoon sugar
1 teaspoon grated fresh ginger
1 tablespoon peanut oil
400g asparagus, trimmed
**1 large brown onion (200g),
sliced thickly**
**2 medium tomatoes (380g),
seeded, chopped coarsely**
**2 teaspoons finely chopped
fresh coriander**
**2 tablespoons roasted
sesame seeds**

1 Combine chicken, garlic, lemon
   grass, sugar, ginger and half of
   the oil in medium bowl.

2 Cut asparagus spears into thirds;
   boil, steam or microwave until
   just tender. Rinse immediately
   under cold water; drain.

3 Heat remaining oil in wok or
   large frying pan. Stir-fry onion
   until just soft; remove from
   wok. Stir-fry chicken mixture,
   in batches, until chicken is
   browned and cooked through.

4 Return chicken mixture and
   onion to wok with asparagus
   and tomato; stir-fry until heated
   through. Serve sprinkled with
   coriander and sesame seeds.

SERVES 4

per serving 14.8g fat; 1186kJ
tip Chicken can be marinated for
up to 3 hours before using.

honey chilli chicken salad

You will need two bunches of asparagus and a quarter of a medium chinese cabbage for this recipe.

500g breast fillets, sliced thinly
1/4 cup (90g) honey
4 red thai chillies, seeded, sliced thinly
1 tablespoon grated fresh ginger
500g asparagus, trimmed
2 tablespoons peanut oil
4 green onions, sliced thinly
1 medium green capsicum (200g), sliced thinly
1 medium yellow capsicum (200g), sliced thinly
1 medium carrot (120g), sliced thinly
150g chinese cabbage, shredded finely
1/3 cup (80ml) lime juice

1 Combine chicken, honey, chilli and ginger in medium bowl.

2 Cut aparagus spears in half; boil, steam or microwave until just tender.
   Rinse immediately under cold water; drain.

3 Meanwhile, heat half of the oil in large wok or frying pan; stir-fry chicken,
   in batches, until browned all over and cooked through.

4 Place chicken and asparagus in large bowl with onion, capsicums, carrot,
   cabbage, juice and remaining oil; toss gently to combine.

SERVES 4

per serving 20.9g fat; 1704kJ

tip A barbecued chicken can also be used; remove and discard bones and skin
then shred meat coarsely before tossing with remaining salad ingredients.

chicken tikka

2 cups (400g) jasmine rice
2 tablespoons tikka
  masala paste
2 tablespoons mango chutney
1kg thigh fillets, sliced thinly
1/3 cup (80ml) vegetable stock
1/2 cup (140g) yogurt
1/2 cup loosely packed, coarsely
  chopped fresh coriander
2 teaspoons lime juice
1 red thai chilli, sliced thinly

1 Cook rice in large saucepan of
  boiling water, uncovered, until
  just tender; drain.

2 Meanwhile, combine paste,
  chutney and chicken in large
  bowl. Heat wok or large frying
  pan; stir-fry chicken mixture,
  in batches, until chicken is
  browned all over.

3 Add remaining ingredients to
  wok; bring to a boil. Reduce
  heat; simmer, uncovered, about
  5 minutes or until chicken is
  cooked through. Serve tikka with
  jasmine rice.

SERVES 4

per serving 23.4g fat; 3293kJ
serving suggestion Top tikka
with extra yogurt, chutney and
fresh coriander leaves.

chicken and chinese broccoli stir-fry

PREPARATION TIME 10 MINUTES • COOKING TIME 15 MINUTES

350g fresh singapore noodles
1 tablespoon peanut oil
750g tenderloins, halved
1 large brown onion (200g),
sliced thickly
3 cloves garlic, crushed
1kg chinese broccoli,
chopped coarsely
1/3 cup (80ml) oyster sauce
1 tablespoon light soy sauce

1 Rinse noodles in strainer under hot water. Separate noodles with fork; drain.

2 Heat half of the oil in wok or large frying pan; stir-fry chicken, in batches, until browned all over and cooked through.

3 Heat remaining oil in same wok; stir-fry onion and garlic until onion softens.

4 Return chicken to wok with broccoli and sauces; stir-fry until broccoli just wilts. Toss chicken mixture with noodles to serve.

SERVES 4

per serving 32.9g fat; 3382kJ
tip Any type of fresh noodle can be used in this recipe.

thai green curry

PREPARATION TIME 10 MINUTES • COOKING TIME 15 MINUTES

1 large brown onion (200g),
    chopped coarsely
2 cloves garlic, crushed
1 tablespoon grated fresh ginger
1 tablespoon finely sliced fresh
    lemon grass
2 tablespoons green curry paste
500g breast fillets,
    sliced thickly
1 tablespoon peanut oil
3/4 cup (180ml) chicken stock
1 2/3 cups (400ml) coconut milk
2 tablespoons lime juice
230g can sliced bamboo
    shoots, drained
300g fresh baby corn, halved
1/2 cup loosely packed, coarsely
    chopped fresh coriander

1 Combine onion, garlic, ginger,
  lemon grass and paste in
  medium bowl. Add chicken; toss
  to coat in mixture. Heat oil in
  wok or large frying pan; stir-fry
  chicken mixture, in batches,
  until chicken is just browned.

2 Return chicken mixture to wok
  with stock, coconut milk and
  juice; cook, uncovered, about
  5 minutes or until curry mixture
  thickens slightly and chicken is
  cooked through.

3 Reduce heat. Add bamboo
  shoots, corn and coriander;
  stir-fry until heated through.

SERVES 4

per serving 37g fat; 2315kJ
serving suggestion Serve this
curry with steamed long-grain
white rice.

chicken penne with mushroom sauce

PREPARATION TIME 10 MINUTES • COOKING TIME 20 MINUTES

375g penne
2 teaspoons olive oil
750g breast fillets,
   chopped coarsely
250g button mushrooms,
   sliced thinly
1/2 cup (125ml) dry white wine
1/3 cup (80ml) tomato juice
3 green onions, sliced thickly
2 small egg tomatoes (120g),
   seeded, sliced thinly

1 Cook pasta in large saucepan of
boiling water, uncovered, until
just tender; drain.

2 Meanwhile, heat oil in wok or
large frying pan; stir-fry chicken,
in batches, until chicken is
browned all over.

3 Place mushrooms in same wok;
stir-fry until tender. Add wine;
bring to a boil. Reduce heat;
simmer, uncovered, 2 minutes.
Return chicken to wok with
juice, onion and tomato;
simmer, uncovered, until sauce
thickens slightly and chicken is
cooked through.

4 Serve pasta topped with chicken
and mushroom sauce.

SERVES 4

per serving 13.8g fat; 2635kJ

tip You can also use elbow
macaroni or shell pasta instead of
the penne.

chicken chermoulla

Chermoulla is a Moroccan blend of herbs and spices traditionally used for preserving or seasoning meat and fish. We use our chermoulla blend here as a quick baste for chicken, but you can also make it for use as a sauce or marinade.

700g thigh fillets, sliced thinly
1/2 cup loosely packed, coarsely chopped fresh flat-leaf parsley
1 tablespoon finely grated lemon rind
1 tablespoon lemon juice
2 teaspoons ground turmeric
1 teaspoon cayenne pepper
1 tablespoon ground coriander
1 medium red onion (170g), chopped finely
2 tablespoons olive oil
1 cup (200g) red lentils
2¹/2 cups (625ml) chicken stock
200g baby spinach leaves
1/2 cup loosely packed, coarsely chopped fresh coriander
1/2 cup loosely packed, coarsely chopped fresh mint
1 tablespoon red wine vinegar
1/3 cup (95g) yogurt

1 Combine chicken, parsley, rind, juice, spices, onion and half of the oil in large bowl. Heat wok or large frying pan; stir-fry chicken mixture, in batches, until chicken is browned and cooked through.

2 Meanwhile, combine lentils and stock in large saucepan. Bring to a boil; reduce heat. Simmer, uncovered, about 8 minutes or until just tender; drain. Place lentils in large bowl with spinach, coriander, mint and combined vinegar and remaining oil; toss gently to combine.

3 Serve chicken mixture on lentil mixture; drizzle with yogurt.

SERVES 4

per serving 24.9g fat; 2191kJ

lentil and pumpkin vindaloo

PREPARATION TIME 10 MINUTES • COOKING TIME 20 MINUTES

³/4 cup (150g) red lentils
500g pumpkin,
    chopped coarsely
1 medium white onion (150g),
    chopped coarsely
1 tablespoon grated
    fresh ginger
2 cloves garlic, crushed
700g thigh fillets, sliced thickly
1 tablespoon peanut oil
¹/4 cup (75g) vindaloo
    curry paste
1²/3 cups (400ml)
    coconut cream
250g baby spinach leaves

1 Cook lentils in large saucepan of
   boiling water, uncovered, until
   just tender; drain. Boil, steam or
   microwave pumpkin until just
   tender; drain.

2 Meanwhile, combine onion,
   ginger and garlic in large bowl.
   Add chicken; toss to coat in
   mixture. Heat oil in wok or large
   frying pan; stir-fry chicken
   mixture, in batches, until
   chicken is just browned.

3 Place curry paste in same wok;
   stir-fry until fragrant. Return
   chicken mixture to wok with
   lentils, pumpkin and coconut
   cream; stir-fry until sauce
   thickens slightly and chicken is
   cooked through.

4 Remove from heat. Add spinach;
   toss gently until spinach
   just wilts.

SERVES 4

per serving 45.2g fat; 2967kJ

tip You can substitute any bottled
curry paste for the fiery vindaloo.

serving suggestion Serve this
spicy curry with steamed jasmine
or basmati rice.

chicken chow mein

PREPARATION TIME 15 MINUTES • COOKING TIME 15 MINUTES

Crispy fried noodles are sold packaged (commonly a 100g packet) already deep-fried and ready to eat. They are sometimes labelled crunchy noodles, and are available in two widths — thin and spaghetti-like or wide and flat like fettuccine. You will need a quarter of a large chinese cabbage for this recipe.

1 tablespoon peanut oil
500g thigh fillets, sliced thinly
2 medium brown onions (300g),
**   sliced thinly**
2 cloves garlic, crushed
1 tablespoon grated
**   fresh ginger**
2 trimmed sticks celery (150g),
**   sliced thinly**
1 medium red capsicum (200g),
**   sliced thinly**
2 teaspoons cornflour
1/2 cup (125ml) chicken stock
1/4 cup (60ml) light soy sauce
5 green onions, sliced thickly
1 cup (80g) bean sprouts
2 cups (160g) finely shredded
**   chinese cabbage**
200g crispy fried noodles

1 Heat half of the oil in wok or large frying pan; stir-fry chicken, in batches, until browned all over and cooked through.

2 Heat remaining oil in same wok; stir-fry brown onion, garlic and ginger until fragrant. Add celery and capsicum; stir-fry until vegetables are just tender.

3 Blend cornflour with stock and sauce in small jug. Return chicken to wok with cornflour mixture; stir-fry until sauce boils and thickens. Add green onion sprouts and cabbage; stir-fry until heated through. Serve on crispy fried noodles.

SERVES 4

per serving 20.4g fat; 1640kJ
tip Prawns can also be added to this recipe.

chicken and bean madras

PREPARATION TIME 10 MINUTES • COOKING TIME 15 MINUTES

1¹/₂ cups (300g) basmati rice
1 tablespoon peanut oil
1 large white onion (200g),
   sliced thinly
700g thigh fillets, sliced thinly
¹/₄ cup (75g) madras
   curry paste
200g green beans,
   chopped coarsely
¹/₂ cup (125ml) chicken stock
1 tablespoon tomato paste

1 Cook rice in large saucepan of boiling water, uncovered, until just tender; drain.

2 Meanwhile, heat oil in wok or large frying pan; stir-fry onion and chicken, in batches, until chicken is just browned.

3 Place curry paste in same wok; stir-fry until fragrant. Return chicken mixture to wok with beans, stock, and tomato paste; stir-fry until sauce thickens slightly and chicken is cooked through. Serve rice with chicken.

SERVES 4

per serving 23.7g fat; 2683kJ

tips You can substitute jasmine rice for the basmati rice.

The curry paste we used contained whole and partially chopped star-anise, which gave this recipe a distinctively spicy flavour.

warm chicken tabbouleh

PREPARATION TIME 15 MINUTES • COOKING TIME 15 MINUTES

Tabbouleh is a traditional Lebanese salad made with a great deal of chopped flat-leaf parsley and varying amounts of burghul, green onion, mint, olive oil and lemon juice.

1 cup (160g) burghul
500g tenderloins, sliced thinly
2 cloves garlic, crushed
¾ cup (180ml) lemon juice
¼ cup (60ml) olive oil
250g cherry tomatoes, halved
4 green onions, chopped coarsely
1 cup loosely packed, coarsely
  chopped fresh flat-leaf parsley
1 cup loosely packed, coarsely
  chopped fresh mint

1 Place burghul in small bowl; cover with boiling water. Stand 15 minutes; drain. Using hands, squeeze out as much excess water as possible.

2 Meanwhile, combine chicken, garlic, a quarter of the juice and 1 tablespoon of the oil in medium bowl; stand 5 minutes. Drain; discard marinade.

3 Heat 1 tablespoon of the oil in wok or large frying pan; stir-fry chicken mixture, in batches, until chicken is browned all over and cooked through. Cover to keep warm.

4 Place burghul with tomato and onion in same wok. Stir-fry until onion softens; remove from heat. Add chicken mixture, parsley, mint, remaining juice and oil; toss gently to combine.

SERVES 4

per serving 21.6g fat; 1843kJ

pork, chicken and rice noodle stir-fry

PREPARATION TIME 10 MINUTES • COOKING TIME 15 MINUTES

You can use fresh or dried rice noodles, wide or spaghetti-like – whatever you prefer.

1/4 cup (55g) sugar
1/3 cup (80ml) mild chilli sauce
1/4 cup (60ml) fish sauce
1 tablespoon light soy sauce
1 tablespoon tomato sauce
500g breast fillets, sliced thickly
150g fresh wide rice noodles
1 tablespoon sesame oil
500g pork mince
1 large brown onion (200g), sliced thickly
2 cloves garlic, crushed
2 cups (160g) bean sprouts
1 cup loosely packed, coarsely chopped fresh coriander
1/3 cup (50g) coarsely chopped roasted peanuts

1 Combine sugar and sauces in large bowl. Add chicken; toss to coat in mixture.

2 Rinse noodles in strainer under hot water. Separate with fork; drain.

3 Meanwhile, drain chicken mixture; reserve marinade. Heat half of the oil in wok or large frying pan; stir-fry chicken mixture, in batches, until chicken is browned all over and cooked through.

4 Heat remaining oil in same wok; stir-fry pork, onion and garlic until pork is cooked through. Return chicken to wok with noodles and reserved marinade. Stir-fry until heated through; remove from heat. Add sprouts, coriander and peanuts; toss gently to combine.

SERVES 4

per serving 27.2g fat; 2707kJ

chicken, vegetable and rice noodle stir-fry

PREPARATION TIME 10 MINUTES • COOKING TIME 10 MINUTES

500g fresh wide rice noodles
1 tablespoon sesame oil
500g breast fillets,
   sliced thinly
250g oyster mushrooms,
   sliced thinly
1/4 cup (60ml) oyster sauce
1 tablespoon fish sauce
1 tablespoon sugar
2 teaspoons sambal oelek
250g baby spinach leaves
1/4 cup loosely packed, coarsely
   chopped fresh coriander

1 Rinse noodles in strainer under hot water. Separate noodles with fork; drain.

2 Meanwhile, heat oil in wok or large frying pan; stir-fry chicken, in batches, until browned all over and cooked through.

3 Place mushrooms in same wok; stir-fry until just tender. Return chicken to wok with noodles, sauces, sugar and sambal oelek; stir-fry until heated through.

4 Remove from heat. Add baby spinach and coriander; toss gently to combine.

SERVES 4

per serving 6.1g fat; 1411kJ
serving suggestion Serve this stir-fry after an appetiser of vegetarian spring rolls.

chicken pitta pockets

PREPARATION TIME 10 MINUTES • COOKING TIME 15 MINUTES

Pitta, a Middle-Eastern flat bread made from white or whole-wheat flour, can be eaten whole, used as a wrapper or cut into wedges and used as dippers.

400g mince
1 clove garlic, crushed
2 teaspoons ground coriander
2 teaspoons ground cumin
1 tablespoon mild chilli sauce
1 tablespoon olive oil
**1 large brown onion (200g),
  sliced thinly**
1/2 cup (80g) pine nuts
**300g spinach, trimmed,
  chopped coarsely**
**1/4 cup loosely packed, coarsely
  chopped fresh mint**
4 pocket pittas
1 cup (280g) yogurt
1 tablespoon lemon juice

1 Combine chicken, garlic, spices and sauce in large bowl.

2 Heat half of the oil in wok or large frying pan; cook chicken mixture until chicken is browned and cooked through. Remove from wok; cover to keep warm.

3 Add remaining oil to same wok; stir-fry onion, pine nuts and spinach until spinach just wilts. Remove from heat. Return chicken mixture to wok with mint; toss gently to combine.

4 Cut pitta pockets in half. Open out each half; spoon in chicken mixture. Drizzle combined yogurt and juice into pitta pockets or serve separately, as desired.

SERVES 4

per serving 38.1g fat; 2936kJ

tip Chilli sauces can vary in degrees of heat – add more or less to suit your taste.

spicy chicken with rice noodles

PREPARATION TIME 10 MINUTES • COOKING TIME 15 MINUTES

750g thigh fillets, chopped coarsely
2 cloves garlic, crushed
2 teaspoons grated fresh ginger
2 teaspoons finely chopped fresh lemon grass
1 tablespoon teriyaki sauce
1 tablespoon sugar
1 teaspoon sambal oelek
1 teaspoon ground cumin
1 teaspoon ground coriander
500g fresh wide rice noodles
2 tablespoons sweet chilli sauce
1 tablespoon peanut oil
500g baby bok choy, quartered

1 Combine chicken, garlic, ginger, lemon grass, teriyaki sauce, sugar, sambal oelek and spices in medium bowl.

2 Rinse noodles in strainer under hot water. Separate with fork; drain. Place noodles in medium bowl; combine with sweet chilli sauce.

3 Meanwhile, heat half of the oil in wok or large frying pan; stir-fry chicken mixture, in batches, until chicken is browned all over and cooked through.

4 Heat remaining oil in same wok; stir-fry bok choy until just wilted.

5 Serve chicken mixture with bok choy and noodles.

SERVES 4

per serving 16g fat; 1727kJ

tip If you can't find fresh rice noodles, the chicken and bok choy can be served on a bed of steamed rice.

sweet soy chicken with noodles

PREPARATION TIME 10 MINUTES • COOKING TIME 20 MINUTES

Kecap manis is an Indonesian sweet soy sauce which is available in most supermarkets and Asian food stores. We used hokkien noodles in this recipe, but any fresh wheat noodle such as shanghai can be substituted. You need a piece of fresh ginger measuring about 1cm in length for this recipe.

500g hokkien noodles
1 tablespoon peanut oil
750g thigh fillets,
**   sliced thickly**
8 green onions,
**   chopped coarsely**
4 cloves garlic, crushed
10g fresh ginger, sliced thinly
230g can sliced water
**   chestnuts, drained**
300g choy sum, trimmed,
**   chopped coarsely**
2 tablespoons coarsely chopped
**   fresh coriander**
2 tablespoons kecap manis
1/4 cup (60ml) chicken stock

1 Rinse noodles in strainer under hot water. Separate noodles with fork; drain.

2 Heat oil in wok or large frying pan; stir-fry chicken, in batches, until browned all over and cooked through. Return chicken to wok with onion, garlic, ginger and water chestnuts; stir-fry until fragrant. Add choy sum, coriander, kecap manis and stock; stir-fry until choy sum just wilts. Top noodles with chicken.

SERVES 4

per serving 19.1g fat; 2030kJ

tips Use chinese broccoli if choy sum is unavailable.

If you can't find kecap manis, substitute it with a mixture of 2 tablespoons of dark soy sauce and 2 tablespoons of brown sugar simmered together in a small saucepan until the sugar dissolves.

serving suggestion Accompany with sambal oelek.

chicken and tamarind stir-fry

PREPARATION TIME 10 MINUTES • COOKING TIME 15 MINUTES

*Tamarind concentrate, a thick, purple-black, ready-to-use sweet-sour paste manufactured from the
pulp of tamarind tree pods, is available from most supermarkets and Asian food stores.*

2 cups (400g) jasmine rice
700g breast fillets,
   sliced thinly
1 tablespoon tamarind
   concentrate
3 cloves garlic, crushed
2 red thai chillies, sliced thinly
2 teaspoons sugar
1 tablespoon lime juice
1 tablespoon peanut oil
1 large brown onion (200g),
   sliced thickly
1/2 cup loosely packed fresh
   coriander leaves

1 Cook rice in large saucepan of
boiling water, uncovered, until
just tender; drain.

2 Meanwhile, combine chicken,
tamarind, garlic, chilli, sugar
and juice in medium bowl.

3 Heat half of the oil in wok or
large frying pan; stir-fry chicken
mixture, in batches, until
browned all over and cooked
through. Heat remaining oil in
same wok; stir-fry onion until
just softened. Return chicken to
wok; toss gently to combine.

4 Serve chicken mixture with rice;
sprinkle with coriander.

SERVES 4

per serving 15.1g fat; 2796kJ
serving suggestion Accompany
with fresh lime wedges.

in the oven

oven-baked parmesan chicken

PREPARATION TIME 10 MINUTES • COOKING TIME 20 MINUTES

Curly endive, also known as frisée, is a loose-headed green vegetable having curly, ragged edged leaves and a slightly bitter flavour. It is usually used as a salad green, but in Europe it is also eaten as a cooked vegetable and in making soups.

1 tablespoon plain flour
2 eggs, beaten lightly
2 cups (140g) stale breadcrumbs
1/3 cup (25g) coarsely grated parmesan cheese
2 tablespoons finely chopped fresh flat-leaf parsley
12 tenderloins (900g)
1 cup firmly packed fresh basil leaves
1/2 cup (125ml) olive oil
1/4 cup (60ml) lemon juice
1 clove garlic, quartered
3/4 cup (120g) kalamata olives, seeded
200g curly endive
40g baby rocket leaves

1 Preheat oven to hot.

2 Combine flour and egg in medium bowl; combine breadcrumbs, cheese and parsley in another medium bowl. Coat chicken, one piece at a time, first in flour mixture then in breadcrumb mixture. Place chicken, in single layer, on oiled oven tray; roast, uncovered, in hot oven about 15 minutes or until chicken is lightly browned and cooked through.

3 Meanwhile, blend or process basil, oil, juice and garlic until dressing is well combined.

4 Serve chicken with combined olives, endive and rocket; drizzle with basil dressing.

SERVES 4

per serving 47.3g fat; 3320kJ

serving suggestion Warm Chicken Tabbouleh (page 27) is another possible accompaniment for this chicken.

crispy mustard tenderloins

PREPARATION TIME 5 MINUTES • COOKING TIME 15 MINUTES

1 cup (300g) mayonnaise
1 tablespoon dijon mustard
1 cup (60g) instant
   potato flakes
12 tenderloins (900g)
150g mesclun
200 cherry tomatoes, halved

1 Preheat oven to moderate.

2 Combine mayonnaise and
   mustard in small bowl; place
   potato flakes in medium shallow
   bowl. Coat chicken, one piece at
   a time, first in mayonnaise
   mixture then in potato flakes.

3 Place chicken, in single layer, on
   oiled oven tray; roast, uncovered,
   in moderate oven for about
   15 minutes or until chicken is
   lightly browned and cooked
   through. Serve chicken with
   combined mesclun and tomato.

SERVES 4

per serving 37.5g fat; 2688kJ

tip Mesclun is a gourmet salad
mixture of assorted young green
leaves, including baby spinach,
mizuna, curly endive and coral
lettuce; substitute baby rocket or
baby spinach leaves if you can't
find mesclun.

chicken schnitzel burgers

PREPARATION TIME 10 MINUTES • COOKING TIME 20 MINUTES

The Germans say that schnitzel should "smell like flowers, be juicy like sherry and crispy like fresh bread" – no wonder it's a dish beloved by cooks everywhere.

4 breast fillets (680g)
1/4 cup (35g) plain flour
2 eggs, beaten lightly
1 tablespoon milk
1/2 cup (80g) corn flake crumbs
1/2 cup (50g) packaged breadcrumbs
2 medium tomatoes (380g),
**   seeded, chopped finely**
1 medium avocado (250g),
**   chopped finely**
2 teaspoons lemon juice
1 long loaf pide
1/2 cup (150g) mayonnaise
1 small white onion (80g),
**   chopped finely**
2 tablespoons french dressing
1 tablespoon sweet fruit chutney
40g baby rocket leaves

1   Preheat oven to hot.

2   Using meat mallet, gently pound chicken between sheets of plastic wrap until 1cm thick.

3   Combine flour, egg and milk in medium bowl; combine corn flakes and breadcrumbs in another medium bowl. Coat chicken, one piece at a time, first in flour mixture then in breadcrumb mixture.

4   Place chicken, in single layer, on oiled oven tray; roast, uncovered, in hot oven, about 20 minutes or until chicken is lightly browned all over and cooked through.

5   Meanwhile, combine tomato, avocado and juice in small bowl. Quarter pide; split pieces horizontally, toast one side lightly. Whisk mayonnaise, onion, dressing and chutney in separate small bowl until well combined.

6   To serve, sandwich rocket, schnitzel, tomato mixture and mayonnaise mixture between two pieces of pide.

SERVES 4

per serving   40.6g fat; 4182kJ

tips   Use stale breadcrumbs instead of corn flake crumbs, and flavour them with grated lemon rind and finely chopped parsley, if preferred.

serving suggestion   Serve with a platter of roasted potato wedges and a bowl of sweet chilli sauce.

in the oven

Cut along both sides of backbone, discard backbone

Using large knife, cut through centre of chicken to halve

Cut between body of chicken and thigh-drumstick

roast chicken with pea mash and gravy

PREPARATION TIME 5 MINUTES • COOKING TIME 25 MINUTES

Who would ever believe you could have a roast chicken on the table in 30 minutes! If you have a microwave oven, it's a speedy and simple process.

1.6kg chicken
1 cup (250ml) chicken stock
3/4 cup (180ml) dry white wine
3 cloves garlic, crushed
2 large potatoes (600g), chopped coarsely
2 1/4 cups (280g) frozen peas
60g butter
2 tablespoons plain flour
1 tablespoon light soy sauce

1 Preheat oven to very hot.

2 Using sharp knife, halve chicken lengthways then cut both halves crossways through the centre (see steps left).

3 Place chicken, skin-side down, in large microwave-safe dish; pour combined stock, wine and garlic over chicken. Microwave, covered, on HIGH for 10 minutes.

4 Carefully remove chicken from microwave-safe dish to serving platter; pour chicken juices into large jug. Place chicken, skin-side up, in single layer, in large baking dish; roast, uncovered, in very hot oven about 15 minutes or until browned all over and cooked through.

5 Meanwhile, boil, steam or microwave potatoes and peas, separately, until just tender; drain. Mash together in large bowl with half of the butter; cover to keep warm.

6 Melt remaining butter in medium saucepan; add flour. Cook, stirring, until mixture thickens and bubbles. Gradually stir in reserved chicken juices; stir until mixture boils and thickens. Stir soy sauce into gravy.

7 Serve pea mash with chicken; top with gravy.

SERVES 4

per serving 45.2g fat; 3099kJ

cajun chicken with creole rice

PREPARATION TIME 10 MINUTES • COOKING TIME 20 MINUTES

1/2 teaspoon salt
2 teaspoons onion powder
3 teaspoons sweet paprika
1 teaspoon freshly ground
  black pepper
1/2 teaspoon chilli powder
4 breast fillets (680g)

CREOLE RICE

1 tablespoon olive oil
1 medium brown onion (150g),
  chopped finely
3 garlic cloves, crushed
1 medium green capsicum
  (200g), chopped finely
1 teaspoon chilli powder
1 teaspoon ground cumin
1 teaspoon ground cinnamon
1 cup (200g) long-grain
  white rice
2 cups (500ml) water
2 tablespoons lime juice
1/4 cup firmly packed, coarsely
  chopped fresh coriander
310g can corn kernels,
  rinsed, drained
420g can red kidney beans,
  rinsed, drained

1 Preheat oven to moderately hot.

2 Combine salt and spices in medium bowl; coat chicken, one piece at a time, in spice mixture.

3 Place chicken, in single layer, on oiled oven tray; roast, uncovered, in moderately hot oven about 20 minutes or until chicken is browned all over and cooked through. Remove chicken from oven; stand 5 minutes, slice thickly.

4 Serve chicken on creole rice; drizzle with pan juices, if any.

creole rice Heat oil in large saucepan; cook onion and garlic, stirring, until onion softens. Add capsicum and spices; cook, stirring, until fragrant. Add rice; stir to combine then add the water. Bring to a boil; reduce heat. Simmer, covered, 15 minutes. Add remaining ingredients; stir until heated through.

SERVES 4

per serving 20.3g fat; 2676kJ

tip To save time, make the creole rice while the chicken is in the oven.

peanut-crusted thai chicken

PREPARATION TIME 10 MINUTES • COOKING TIME 20 MINUTES

1 cup (150g) roasted
   unsalted peanuts
1/4 cup (75g) red curry paste
1 tablespoon kecap manis
1/2 cup (125ml) coconut milk
1 cup loosely packed coarsely
   chopped fresh coriander
4 breast fillets (680g)
1 telegraph cucumber (400g)
2 cups (160g) bean sprouts
1/3 cup loosely packed, coarsely
   chopped fresh mint
1 medium red onion (170g),
   halved, sliced thinly
1 teaspoon fish sauce
2 tablespoons sweet chilli sauce
1 tablespoon lime juice
1 tablespoon peanut oil

1 Preheat oven to moderately hot.

2 Blend or process peanuts, paste, kecap manis, coconut milk and half of the coriander until just combined.

3 Place chicken, in single layer, on oiled oven tray; spread peanut mixture on each piece. Roast, uncovered, in moderately hot oven about 20 minutes or until chicken is cooked through. Remove chicken from oven; stand 5 minutes, slice thickly.

4 Meanwhile, cut cucumber in half lengthways. Remove and discard seeds; slice thinly. Combine cucumber in large bowl with sprouts, mint, onion and remaining coriander.

5 Combine sauces, juice and oil in screw-top jar; shake well. Pour dressing over cucumber salad; toss gently to combine. Serve chicken with salad.

SERVES 4

per serving 44.6g fat; 2749kJ

tip The reason you rest chicken after removing it from the oven is to let the juices settle, making it is easier to slice.

tandoori drumettes with cucumber raita

PREPARATION TIME 5 MINUTES • COOKING TIME 20 MINUTES

Drumettes are in fact wings trimmed to resemble drumsticks; in some areas, this name is used (along with lovely legs) when describing pared-back and trimmed drumsticks. You can use either in this recipe.

**2 cups (400g) jasmine rice
2 tablespoons tandoori paste
400g yogurt
12 drumettes (960g)
1 lebanese cucumber (130g),
    seeded, chopped finely
1 tablespoon finely chopped
    fresh mint
1 teaspoon ground cumin**

1 Preheat oven to moderately hot.

2 Cook rice in large saucepan of boiling water, uncovered, until just tender; drain.

3 Meanwhile, combine paste and half of the yogurt in large bowl. Add chicken; toss until chicken is well coated. Place chicken, in single layer, on wire oven rack over baking dish; roast chicken, uncovered, in moderately hot oven about 20 minutes or until chicken is browned all over and cooked through.

4 Combine remaining yogurt with cucumber, mint and cumin in small bowl. Serve rice topped with tandoori chicken and cucumber raita.

SERVES 4

per serving 20g fat; 2800kJ

tip Raita is a fresh yogurt salad that goes extremely well with spicy Indian dishes.

chicken and corn tartlets

PREPARATION TIME 15 MINUTES • COOKING TIME 15 MINUTES

1 tablespoon olive oil
1 medium brown onion (150g),
    chopped finely
2 cloves garlic, crushed
375g mince
1 tablespoon coarsely chopped
    fresh chives
2 tablespoons coarsely chopped
    fresh flat-leaf parsley
125g can creamed corn
1/2 cup (35g) stale breadcrumbs
2 sheets ready-rolled
    puff pastry
1 egg, beaten lightly

1 Preheat oven to hot.

2 Heat oil in small frying pan;
  cook onion and garlic, stirring,
  until onion softens.

3 Combine onion mixture in
  medium bowl with chicken,
  chives, parsley, creamed corn
  and breadcrumbs.

4 Halve pastry sheets; divide
  chicken among pastry pieces,
  leaving 2cm edge. Brush around
  pastry edges with egg; fold
  edges inward, brush folded
  edges with egg.

5 Bake tartlets, uncovered, in hot
  oven about 15 minutes or until
  pastry is lightly browned and
  chicken mixture cooked through.

SERVES 4

per serving 33g fat; 2423kJ
serving suggestion Sprinkle tops
of tarlets with fresh chives and
serve with a fresh garden salad.

*Divide chicken mixture among pastry pieces
leaving 2cm edge*

Brush folded edges with egg

chicken, asparagus and potatoes in garlic cream sauce

PREPARATION TIME 5 MINUTES • COOKING TIME 25 MINUTES

Kipfler potatoes, small and finger-shaped, have a nutty flavour and are great baked or in salads.

**500g kipfler potatoes,
  halved lengthways**
1 teaspoon cracked black pepper
1 tablespoon olive oil
4 breast fillets (680g)
500g asparagus, trimmed
**6 slices prosciutto (90g),
  chopped coarsely**
1 clove garlic, crushed
1/2 cup (125ml) dry white wine
2 tablespoons seeded mustard
300ml cream
**1/4 cup loosely packed coarsely
  chopped fresh chives**

1 Preheat oven to hot.

2 Combine potato, pepper and oil in large bowl; mix well. Place potato, in single layer, on oiled oven tray; roast, uncovered, in hot oven about 20 minutes or until browned.

3 Meanwhile, heat large lightly oiled frying pan; cook chicken, in batches, until browned both sides. Place chicken, in single layer, on oven tray; roast, uncovered, in hot oven with potatoes about 10 minutes or until cooked through. Remove chicken from oven; cover. Stand 5 minutes; slice thickly.

4 Meanwhile, boil, steam or microwave asparagus until just tender; drain. Cover to keep warm.

5 Cook prosciutto in same pan, stirring, until just crisp. Remove from pan; cover to keep warm. Add garlic to pan; cook, stirring over low heat, until fragrant. Add wine; bring to a boil. Boil, stirring, until reduced to about 2 tablespoons. Add mustard and cream; bring to a boil. Boil, stirring, until mixture thickens slightly. Stir in chives.

6 Divide asparagus among serving plates; top with potato, half of the prosciutto, chicken, sauce, then remaining prosciutto.

SERVES 4

per serving 48.4g fat; 3039kJ

supreme pizza

PREPARATION TIME 10 MINUTES • COOKING TIME 15 MINUTES

Ready-made pizza bases are available in all supermarkets and fresh ones can be found at some bakeries. You need to purchase a large barbecued chicken weighing approximately 900g for this recipe.

25cm (335g) ready-made pizza base
2 tablespoons barbecue sauce
1 small brown onion (80g), sliced thinly
1 small tomato (130g), chopped coarsely
1¹/₂ cups (200g) coarsely chopped chicken
100g button mushrooms, sliced thinly
¹/₂ cup (75g) sun-dried tomatoes in oil, drained, chopped coarsely
¹/₄ cup (30g) seeded black olives
1 cup (110g) pizza cheese
¹/₄ cup loosely packed basil leaves

1 Preheat oven to hot.

2 Place pizza base on oven tray; spread with sauce. Top with onion, tomato, chicken, mushrooms, sun-dried tomato, olives and cheese.

3 Bake, uncovered, in hot oven about 15 minutes or until pizza top browns and base is crisp.

4 Serve pizza sprinkled with basil.

SERVES 4

per serving 13.5g fat; 1962kJ

tip Pizza cheese is a blend of coarsely grated processed cheddar, mozarella and parmesan cheeses available from your supermarket.

serving suggestion Accompany with a fresh garden salad dressed in a garlic vinaigrette.

mexi-wings with cherry tomato salsa

PREPARATION TIME 5 MINUTES • COOKING TIME 25 MINUTES

You need to purchase two punnets of cherry tomatoes for this recipe.

8 large wings (1kg)
2 x 35g packets taco
   seasoning mix
2 tablespoons tomato sauce
1 tablespoon vegetable oil
1/3 cup (80ml) lime juice
500g cherry tomatoes
2 medium avocados (500g),
   chopped coarsely
310g can corn kernels, drained
1 medium red onion (170g),
   chopped finely
1/4 cup firmly packed fresh
   coriander leaves

1 Preheat oven to moderately hot.

2 Combine chicken, seasoning,
   sauce, oil and 1 tablespoon of
   the juice in large bowl; toss to
   coat chicken all over.

3 Place chicken, in single layer, in
   large shallow oiled baking dish;
   roast, uncovered, in moderately
   hot oven about 25 minutes or
   until chicken is browned all over
   and cooked through.

4 Meanwhile, quarter tomatoes;
   combine in medium bowl with
   avocado, corn, onion, coriander
   and remaining juice.

5 Serve salsa topped with wings.

   SERVES 4

   per serving 34.2g fat; 2440kJ

satay drumettes

PREPARATION TIME 5 MINUTES • COOKING TIME 25 MINUTES

Drumettes are in fact wings trimmed to resemble drumsticks; in some areas, this name is used (along with lovely legs) when describing pared-back and trimmed drumsticks. You can use either in this recipe.

12 drumettes (960g)
¼ cup (60ml) kecap manis
2 cups (400g) jasmine rice
¾ cup (210g) crunchy peanut butter
⅔ cup (160ml) chicken stock
2 tablespoons sweet chilli sauce
1 tablespoon light soy sauce
1 tablespoon lemon juice
1 cup (250ml) coconut milk

1 Preheat oven to hot.

2 Place chicken, in single layer, in large shallow oiled baking dish; brush chicken all over with kecap manis. Roast, uncovered, in hot oven about 25 minutes or until chicken is cooked through.

3 Meanwhile, cook rice in large saucepan of boiling water, uncovered, until just tender; drain. Cover to keep warm.

4 Combine peanut butter, stock, sauces, juice and coconut milk in medium saucepan; bring to a boil. Reduce heat; simmer, uncovered, 5 minutes.

5 Serve rice and chicken drizzled with satay sauce.

SERVES 4

per serving 54.8g fat; 4336kJ
tip You can also cook the drumettes on a grill or barbecue.

sticky barbecue wings

PREPARATION TIME 10 MINUTES • COOKING TIME 20 MINUTES

**2 cups (400g) long-grain
  white rice**
12 wings (1kg)
¹/₄ cup (60ml) barbecue sauce
¹/₄ cup (60ml) plum sauce
1 tablespoon worcestershire sauce

1 Preheat oven to hot.

2 Cook rice in large saucepan of boiling water, uncovered, until just tender; drain. Cover to keep warm.

3 Meanwhile, cut wing tips from chicken; cut wings in half at joint.

4 Combine sauces in large bowl. Add chicken; toss to coat chicken all over. Place chicken, in single layer, in large oiled baking dish; roast, uncovered, in hot oven about 20 minutes or until chicken is cooked through. Serve chicken with rice.

SERVES 4

per serving 9g fat; 2674kJ

serving suggestion Accompany with a homemade coleslaw dressed in a red wine vinaigrette.

Cut wing tips from pieces

Cut wings in half at joint

on the grill

chicken ratatouille

PREPARATION TIME 10 MINUTES • COOKING TIME 15 MINUTES

4 breast fillets (680g)
1 tablespoon olive oil
1 medium brown onion (150g), chopped finely
1 medium yellow capsicum (200g), chopped coarsely
1 medium red capsicum (200g), chopped coarsely
1 medium eggplant (300g), chopped coarsely
1 tablespoon tomato paste
3 small zucchini (270g), chopped coarsely
700g jar tomato pasta sauce
$1/2$ cup (125ml) chicken stock
1 cup loosely packed, coarsely chopped fresh basil
4 basil leaves

1 Preheat oven to hot. Using meat mallet, gently pound chicken between sheets of plastic wrap until 2cm thick. Cook chicken, in batches, on heated oiled grill plate (or grill or barbecue) until chicken is browned both sides and cooked through.

2 Meanwhile, heat oil in medium saucepan; cook onion, stirring, until onion softens. Add capsicums, eggplant and paste; cook, stirring, 2 minutes. Add zucchini; cook, stirring, 2 minutes. Add sauce and stock; bring to a boil. Reduce heat; simmer, covered, 8 minutes, stirring occasionally. Uncover; cook 3 minutes. Remove from heat; stir in chopped basil.

3 Serve chicken with ratatouille; top with whole basil leaves.

SERVES 4

per serving 15.8g fat; 1722kJ
serving suggestion Serve with your favourite pasta.

char-grilled chicken with warm tomato salad

PREPARATION TIME 15 MINUTES • COOKING TIME 15 MINUTES

4 breast fillets (680g)
2 tablespoons lime juice
1/4 cup (60ml) sweet
**   chilli sauce**
2 cloves garlic, crushed
4 fresh kaffir lime
**   leaves, shredded**
20g butter
2 medium brown onions
**   (300g), sliced thickly**
2 tablespoons red wine vinegar
1/4 cup (55g) sugar
2 tablespoons sweet
**   chilli sauce, extra**
1/4 cup (60ml) water
1/4 cup (60ml) orange juice
6 medium egg tomatoes
**   (450g), cut into wedges**
1 tablespoon bottled jalapeño
**   chillies, chopped coarsely**
3 green onions, sliced thickly

1 Combine chicken, juice, sauce, garlic and leaves in large bowl; toss to coat chicken in mixture.

2 Heat butter in large saucepan; cook brown onion, stirring, until just softened. Add vinegar and sugar; cook, stirring, 2 minutes. Stir in extra sauce, the water and juice; add tomato and chilli, stir until heated through.

3 Cook drained chicken, in batches, on heated oiled grill plate (or grill or barbecue) until browned both sides and cooked through. Cover to keep warm.

4 Serve chicken on warm tomato salad; top with green onion.

SERVES 4

per serving 14.5g fat; 1674kJ

pesto chicken salad

PREPARATION TIME 5 MINUTES • COOKING TIME 15 MINUTES

1/3 cup (90g) basil pesto
2 tablespoons balsamic vinegar
4 breast fillets (680g)
6 medium egg tomatoes
   (450g), halved
125g baby rocket leaves
1 tablespoon olive oil

1 Combine pesto and vinegar in small bowl.

2 Place chicken and tomato on large tray; brush half of the pesto mixture over both.

3 Cook tomato on heated oiled grill plate (or grill or barbecue) until just softened; remove from plate. Cook chicken on same grill plate until browned both sides and cooked through. Stand 5 minutes; slice thickly.

4 Place tomato and chicken in large bowl with rocket. Add oil and remaining pesto mixture; toss gently to combine.

SERVES 4

per serving 23.2g fat; 1607kJ

tip You can substitute mixed lettuce leaves for the baby rocket.

serving suggestion Sprinkle with shaved parmesan cheese.

angel hair pasta, chicken and rocket

PREPARATION TIME 5 MINUTES • COOKING TIME 25 MINUTES

250g angel hair pasta
1 tablespoon olive oil
1 medium brown onion (150g),
   chopped finely
750g mince
1 tablespoon tomato paste
700g bottled tomato pasta sauce
2 teaspoons dried basil
80g rocket
2 tablespoons finely grated
   parmesan cheese
250g coarsely grated
   mozzarella cheese

1 Cook pasta in large saucepan of boiling water, uncovered, until just tender; drain.

2 Meanwhile, heat oil in large saucepan; cook onion, stirring, until just softened. Add chicken; cook, stirring, 4 minutes. Add paste; cook, stirring, until chicken is cooked through. Add sauce; cook, stirring, 5 minutes. Remove from heat; stir in basil.

3 Place half of the pasta in lightly oiled 2-litre (8-cup) ovenproof dish. Top with half of the chicken mixture, rocket and parmesan; repeat with remaining pasta and chicken mixture. Top with mozzarella; place under preheated grill about 2 minutes or until mozzarella just browns.

SERVES 4

per serving 36.9g fat; 3508kJ

tip Toss a little olive oil through pasta to keep the strands from sticking together.

serving suggestion Serve with a crisp green salad.

Oil keeps the drained pasta from sticking together and becoming clumpy

Top the rocket and parmesan layer with remaining pasta

sweet and sour chicken

PREPARATION TIME 10 MINUTES • COOKING TIME 10 MINUTES

4 breast fillets (680g)
440g can pineapple pieces in
  natural juice
1 tablespoon peanut oil
1 small brown onion (80g),
  sliced thinly
1 large red capsicum (350g),
  chopped coarsely
1 large green capsicum (350g),
  chopped coarsely
1 trimmed stick celery (75g),
  sliced thickly
1/4 cup (60ml) tomato sauce
1/4 cup (60ml) plum sauce
2 tablespoons light soy sauce
1/4 cup (60ml) white vinegar
1 tablespoon cornflour
1/2 cup (125ml) chicken stock

1 Cook chicken, in batches, on heated oiled grill plate (or grill or barbecue) until browned all over and cooked through. Stand 5 minutes; slice thickly. Cover to keep warm.

2 Meanwhile, drain pineapple; reserve juice. Heat oil in large saucepan; cook pineapple, onion, capsicums and celery, stirring, 4 minutes. Add reserved juice, sauces, vinegar and blended cornflour and stock; stir until mixture boils and thickens.

3 Serve chicken topped with sweet and sour sauce.

SERVES 4

per serving 14.5g fat; 1795kJ
serving suggestion Serve with steamed jasmine rice.

kebabs with pawpaw salsa

PREPARATION TIME 10 MINUTES • COOKING TIME 15 MINUTES

Soak 12 bamboo skewers in water before using to avoid their scorching and splintering.

12 tenderloins (900g)
1 small pawpaw (650g),
  peeled, seeded
4 green onions, sliced thinly
1 lebanese cucumber, seeded,
  chopped coarsely
1/2 cup firmly packed, coarsely
  chopped fresh mint
2 teaspoons grated fresh ginger
1 tablespoon sweet chilli sauce
2 tablespoons lime juice

1 Thread chicken onto skewers.
   Cook skewers, in batches, on
   heated oiled grill plate (or grill
   or barbecue) about 15 minutes
   or until chicken is browned all
   over and cooked through.

2 Meanwhile, chop pawpaw finely.
   Place in small bowl with onion,
   cucumber, mint, ginger, sauce
   and juice; toss gently to combine.

3 Serve kebabs topped with salsa.

   SERVES 4

   per serving 1.6g fat; 322kJ

   tip You can substitute mango for
   the pawpaw if you like.

   serving suggestion Warm large
   pieces of pitta bread or flour
   tortillas to serve with the kebabs.

Weave the chicken into skewers

Use a small spoon to seed the pawpaw

chicken tenderloins in green peppercorn and tarragon dressing

PREPARATION TIME 10 MINUTES • COOKING TIME 15 MINUTES

2 tablespoons water
2 teaspoons drained green peppercorns, crushed
2 teaspoons seeded mustard
2 green onions, sliced thinly
1 tablespoon coarsely chopped fresh tarragon
1 tablespoon olive oil
1 tablespoon sugar
1/3 cup (80ml) white wine vinegar
4 medium potatoes (800g)
8 tenderloins (600g)
1 tablespoon cracked black pepper
4 large tomatoes (1kg), sliced thinly
1 medium red onion (170g), sliced thinly

1 Combine the water, peppercorn, mustard, green onion, tarragon, oil, sugar and vinegar in small bowl. Whisk to combine dressing; reserve.

2 Boil, steam or microwave potato until just tender; drain.

3 Meanwhile, coat chicken all over in pepper; cook chicken, in batches, on heated oiled grill plate (or grill or barbecue) until browned both sides and cooked through. Stand 5 minutes; slice thickly.

4 When potatoes are cool enough to handle, slice thickly. Cook potato, in batches, on same heated oiled grill plate until browned both sides.

5 Arrange chicken, potato, tomato and onion slices on serving plates; drizzle with reserved dressing.

SERVES 4

per serving 13.4g fat; 1791kJ

mexican burgers

PREPARATION TIME 10 MINUTES • COOKING TIME 10 MINUTES

450g mince
35g packet taco seasoning mix
1/3 cup (80g) sour cream
1 tablespoon finely chopped
   fresh coriander
4 sourdough rolls, halved
1 medium avocado (250g),
   sliced thinly
1/3 cup (85g) medium
   chunky salsa

1 Using hand, combine chicken
  and seasoning in large bowl.
  Divide mixture into quarters;
  using hands, form each portion
  into burger shape. Cook burgers
  on heated oiled grill plate (or
  grill or barbecue) until browned
  both sides and cooked through.

2 Meanwhile, combine sour cream
  and coriander in small bowl.

3 Toast rolls, cut-side up, under
  hot grill. Spread half of each roll
  with cream mixture; top each
  with burger, avocado, salsa and
  remaining half of roll.

SERVES 4

per serving 29.9g fat; 2288kJ

tip Salsa comes in mild, medium
and hot flavours; use whichever
heat level you like.

serving suggestion Char-grilled
eggplant or zucchini could be
added as a burger topping.

chicken with cucumber and tomato salsa

PREPARATION TIME 10 MINUTES • COOKING TIME 15 MINUTES

4 breast fillets (680g)
2 small tomatoes (260g),
  seeded, sliced thinly
1 lebanese cucumber (130g),
  seeded, sliced thinly
1 small red onion (100g),
  halved, sliced thinly
2 tablespoons sweet
  chilli sauce
3 teaspoons lime juice
1 tablespoon coarsely chopped
  fresh coriander

1 Cook chicken, in batches, on heated oiled grill plate (or grill or barbecue) until browned both sides and cooked through.

2 Meanwhile, combine remaining ingredients in small bowl; toss gently to combine. Serve chicken topped with salsa.

SERVES 4

per serving 9.7g fat; 1075kJ
serving suggestion Grill a few wedges of lime after you grill the chicken to serve with this recipe.

mustard and rosemary chicken

PREPARATION TIME 5 MINUTES • COOKING TIME 15 MINUTES

You need two lemons for this recipe.

4 breast fillets (680g)
1 tablespoon seeded mustard
1 tablespoon lemon juice
1 tablespoon olive oil
1 tablespoon finely chopped
**   fresh rosemary**
1 clove garlic, crushed
600g tiny new potatoes,
**   quartered**
250g baby spinach leaves
20g butter
1 lemon (140g), quartered

1 Combine chicken, mustard, juice, oil, rosemary and garlic in medium bowl; toss to coat chicken in mustard mixture.

2 Cook chicken, in batches, on heated oiled grill plate (or grill or barbecue) cook until chicken is browned both sides and cooked through.

3 Meanwhile, boil, steam or microwave potato until just tender; drain. Place hot potato in large bowl with spinach and butter; toss gently until butter melts and spinach just wilts.

4 Serve chicken with vegetables and lemon quarters.

SERVES 4

per serving 18.5g fat; 1774kJ

thai chicken and rice

PREPARATION TIME 5 MINUTES • COOKING TIME 15 MINUTES

**2 cups (300g) long-grain
   white rice**
**1 cup firmly packed fresh
   mint leaves**
**¹/₃ cup (80ml) sweet
   chilli sauce**
1 tablespoon fish sauce
1 tablespoon soy sauce
¹/₂ cup (125ml) lime juice
2 teaspoons grated fresh ginger
**¹/₄ cup coarsely chopped fresh
   lemon grass**
4 breast fillets (680g)
**1 small red capsicum (150g),
   chopped finely**

1 Cook rice in large saucepan of
   boiling water, uncovered, until
   just tender; drain.

2 Reserve 2 tablespoons of the
   mint; blend or process remaining
   mint with sauces, juice, ginger
   and lemon grass until smooth.

3 Cook chicken, in batches, on
   heated oiled grill plate (or grill
   or barbecue) until browned both
   sides and cooked through.

4 Toss capsicum through cooked
   rice. Divide among serving
   plates; top with chicken. Drizzle
   with sauce; sprinkle with
   reserved coarsely chopped mint.

SERVES 4

per serving 10.6g fat; 2275kJ
serving suggestion If you like
your curry hot, add one finely
chopped red thai chilli to the
mint mixture.

coriander and chilli grilled fillets

PREPARATION TIME 10 MINUTES • COOKING TIME 15 MINUTES

6 thigh fillets (660g), halved

CORIANDER CHILLI SAUCE

8 green onions, chopped coarsely
3 cloves garlic, quartered
3 red thai chillies, seeded, chopped coarsely
1/4 cup loosely packed fresh coriander leaves
1 teaspoon sugar
1 tablespoon fish sauce
1/4 cup (60ml) lime juice

CHICKPEA SALAD

2 x 300g cans chickpeas, rinsed, drained
2 medium egg tomatoes (150g), chopped coarsely
2 green onions, chopped finely
2 tablespoons lime juice
1 cup loosely packed, coarsely chopped fresh coriander
1 tablespoon olive oil

1 Cook chicken, in batches, on heated oiled grill plate (or grill or barbecue) until almost cooked through. Brush about two-thirds of the coriander chilli sauce all over chicken; cook further 5 minutes or until chicken is cooked through.

2 Serve chicken, sprinkled with remaining coriander chilli sauce, with chickpea salad.

coriander chilli sauce Blend or process onion, garlic, chilli, coriander and sugar until finely chopped. Add fish sauce and juice; blend until well combined.

chickpea salad Combine ingredients in large bowl; toss to combine.

SERVES 4

per serving 18.8g fat; 1659kJ

chicken, cashew and mesclun salad

PREPARATION TIME 5 MINUTES • COOKING TIME 15 MINUTES

4 breast fillets (680g)
1/2 cup (125ml) dry white wine
1/2 cup (125ml) water
1/2 cup (125ml) sweet
**   chilli sauce**
1 cup (150g) unsalted
**   roasted cashews**
100g mesclun
1/2 cup (125ml) ranch dressing

1 Cook chicken, in batches, on heated oiled grill plate (or grill or barbecue) until browned both sides and cooked through. Stand 5 minutes; slice thickly. Cover to keep warm.

2 Meanwhile, bring wine to a boil in small saucepan; boil, uncovered, until reduced by two-thirds. Add the water and sauce; cook, stirring, until sauce boils and thickens slightly. Add nuts; cook, stirring, until nuts are coated in sauce.

3 Combine chicken in large bowl with mesclun. Top with nuts; drizzle with dressing.

SERVES 4

per serving 38.2g fat; 2633kJ

tip If you can't find ranch dressing, you can substitute it with a good quality mayonnaise, thinned with a little lemon juice and water.

lemon basil chicken on hot potato salad

PREPARATION TIME 10 MINUTES • COOKING TIME 15 MINUTES

4 thigh cutlets (640g)
2 cloves garlic, crushed
2 tablespoons lemon juice
1 teaspoon cracked
    black pepper
1/2 cup coarsely chopped
    fresh basil
5 slices pancetta (75g)
500g tiny new potatoes, halved
1/4 cup (60g) sour cream
1/4 cup (75g) mayonnaise
2 tablespoons drained green
    peppercorns, chopped coarsely
2 tablespoons french dressing

1 Combine chicken, garlic, juice,
   pepper and half of the basil in
   medium bowl; toss to coat
   chicken all over in marinade.

2 Cook chicken, in batches, on
   heated oiled grill plate (or grill or
   barbecue), brushing occasionally
   with marinade, until chicken is
   browned all over and cooked
   through. Cover to keep warm.

3 Cook pancetta on heated oiled
   grill plate (or grill or barbecue)
   about 1 minute each side or
   until crisp; chop coarsely.

4 Meanwhile, boil, steam or
   microwave potato until just
   tender; drain. Divide potato
   among serving plates; drizzle
   with combined sour cream,
   mayonnaise, peppercorns,
   dressing, remaining basil and
   pancetta. Serve grilled chicken
   with hot potato salad.

SERVES 4

per serving 25.2g fat; 1822kJ

tandoori chicken salad with pappadums

PREPARATION TIME 10 MINUTES • COOKING TIME 10 MINUTES

Pappadums are sun-dried crispbreads made from a combination of lentil and rice flours, oil and spices.

10 tenderloins (750g)
200g yogurt
2 tablespoons tandoori paste
8 pappadums
200g mesclun
4 large egg tomatoes (360g),
chopped coarsely
2 lebanese cucumbers (260g),
seeded, sliced thinly
1 small red onion (100g),
sliced thinly

DRESSING

¼ cup (60ml) vegetable oil
¼ cup (60ml) lime juice
2 tablespoons hot
mango chutney

1 Combine chicken, yogurt and paste in large bowl; toss to coat chicken in tandoori mixture.

2 Cook chicken, in batches, on heated oiled grill plate (or grill or barbecue), until browned all over and cooked through. Stand 5 minutes; slice thickly.

3 Meanwhile, place 2 pappadums on edge of microwave-safe plate. Cook on HIGH about 30 seconds or until puffed; repeat with remaining pappadums.

4 Combine chicken in large bowl with mesclun, tomato, cucumber, onion and dressing; toss gently. Serve salad with pappadums.

dressing Combine ingredients in screw-top jar; shake well.

SERVES 4

per serving 28g fat; 2193kJ

portuguese-style chicken thighs

PREPARATION TIME 15 MINUTES • COOKING TIME 15 MINUTES

2 teaspoons cracked
   black pepper
2 red thai chillies, seeded,
   chopped finely
1/2 teaspoon hot paprika
1 clove garlic, crushed
1 teaspoon finely grated
   orange rind
1/4 cup (60ml) orange juice
2 tablespoons red wine vinegar
1/4 cup (60ml) olive oil
6 thigh fillets (660g), halved
2 medium oranges (480g),
   peeled, segmented
250g baby spinach leaves
1 medium red onion (170g),
   sliced thinly

1 Combine pepper, chilli, paprika, garlic, rind, juice, vinegar and oil in medium bowl. Reserve about a quarter of the spicy dressing in small jug; use hands to rub remaining spicy dressing into chicken pieces.

2 Cook chicken, in batches, on heated oiled grill plate (or grill or barbecue) until browned both sides and cooked through.

3 Toss orange segments, spinach and onion in large bowl. Divide among serving plates; top with chicken. Drizzle with reserved spicy dressing.

SERVES 4

per serving 24.9g fat; 1647kJ
serving suggestion Serve with slices of crusty bread.

chicken and crunchy noodle salad

PREPARATION TIME 5 MINUTES • COOKING TIME 15 MINUTES

Crispy fried noodles are sold packaged (commonly a 100g packet) already deep-fried and ready to eat. They're sometimes labelled crunchy noodles and are available in two widths – thin and spaghetti-like, or wide and flat like fettuccine.

4 breast fillets (680g)
500g baby bok choy,
  shredded coarsely
250g cherry tomatoes, halved
50g fresh shiitake mushrooms,
  sliced thinly
1/4 cup firmly packed fresh
  coriander leaves
1 cup (80g) bean sprouts
3 green onions, sliced thinly
1/3 cup (80ml) light soy sauce
1 teaspoon sesame oil
2 tablespoons dry sherry
100g crispy fried noodles

1 Cook chicken, in batches, on heated oiled grill plate (or grill or barbecue) until browned both sides and cooked through. Stand 5 minutes; slice thinly.

2 Meanwhile, combine bok choy, tomato, mushrooms, coriander, sprouts and onion in large bowl.

3 Combine sauce, oil and sherry in screw-top jar; shake well.

4 Combine noodles with chicken bok choy mixture and dressing; toss gently to combine.

SERVES 4

per serving 14g fat; 1444kJ
tip The dressing should be added just before serving.

burger with the lot

PREPARATION TIME 10 MINUTES • COOKING TIME 15 MINUTES

750g mince
1 egg
35g packet taco seasoning mix
¹/₃ cup (35g) packaged
breadcrumbs
1 medium brown onion (150g),
sliced thinly
4 hamburger buns
1 baby cos lettuce
1 small tomato (130g),
sliced thinly
4 large slices canned
beetroot, drained
1 small avocado (200g),
sliced thinly
4 slices cheddar cheese

1 Using hand, combine chicken, egg, seasoning and breadcrumbs in large bowl. Divide mixture into quarters; using hands, form each portion into burger shape.

2 Cook burgers on heated oiled grill plate (or grill or barbecue) until browned both sides and cooked through. Meanwhile, cook onion on grill plate alongside burgers, stirring, until softened and lightly browned.

3 Split buns in half; toast, cut-side up, until lightly browned.

4 Sandwich lettuce, tomato, beetroot, avocado, burger, cheese and onion in toasted buns.

SERVES 4

per serving 34.1g fat; 2834kJ
serving suggestion You can add bacon or your favourite sauce to the filling.

take one barbecued chicken...

chicken wraps

PREPARATION TIME 15 MINUTES • COOKING TIME 5 MINUTES

You need to purchase a large barbecued chicken weighing approximately 900g for this recipe.

1 large tomato (500g), chopped coarsely
1 medium avocado (500g), chopped coarsely
1 small red onion (100g), chopped coarsely
2 tablespoons coarsely chopped fresh coriander
1/2 cup (130g) medium chunky salsa
4 cups (400g) shredded chicken
8 large flour tortillas

1 Combine tomato, avocado, onion, coriander, salsa and chicken in large bowl.

2 Heat one tortilla in microwave on HIGH about 20 seconds or until just flexible. Top tortilla with about an an eighth of the chicken filling; roll to enclose filling. Repeat with remaining tortillas and chicken filling.

SERVES 4

per serving 29.9g fat; 2262kJ

tip Store the remaining uncooked tortillas, sealed tightly, in the refrigerator or freezer.

serving suggestion Tie each wrap with the top end of a green onion made pliable by soaking it briefly in hot water.

lemon ginger chicken

PREPARATION TIME 5 MINUTES • COOKING TIME 15 MINUTES

You need to purchase a large barbecued chicken weighing approximately 900g for this recipe.

2 cups (400g) long-grain white rice
2 teaspoons olive oil
1 tablespoon grated fresh ginger
2 tablespoons honey
2 teaspoons cornflour
1/2 cup (125ml) water
1/4 cup (60ml) lemon juice
1 tablespoon light soy sauce
1 tablespoon sweet chilli sauce
1 large (900g) barbecued chicken, quartered

1 Cook rice in large saucepan of boiling water, uncovered, until just tender; drain.

2 Meanwhile, heat oil in large frying pan; cook ginger and honey, stirring, 1 minute. Blend cornflour with the water in small jug; stir into pan with juice and sauces. Cook, stirring, until mixture boils and thickens. Add chicken; reduce heat. Simmer, uncovered, 5 minutes, turning chicken once during cooking. Serve chicken with rice.

SERVES 4

per serving 22.3g fat; 3001kJ

curried chicken and mushroom pies

PREPARATION TIME 10 MINUTES • COOKING TIME 15 MINUTES

You need to purchase a large barbecued chicken weighing approximately 900g for this recipe.

1 sheet ready-rolled puff pastry
1 tablespoon vegetable oil
400g button mushrooms,
    sliced thickly
1 clove garlic, crushed
2 teaspoons curry powder
1/2 cup (125ml) chicken stock
3/4 cup (180ml) cream
4 cups (400g) shredded chicken
1/2 teaspoon cracked
    black pepper
6 green onions, sliced thinly

1 Preheat oven to hot. Cut pastry into four equal squares; score top of each square in crosshatch pattern with sharp knife. Place on oiled oven tray; bake, uncovered, in hot oven about 10 minutes or until pastry puffs and browns. Cool; split pastry puffs in half through the centre.

2 Meanwhile, heat oil in large saucepan; cook mushrooms, garlic and curry powder, stirring, until mushrooms are tender. Stir in stock and cream; cook, stirring, about 5 minutes or until mixture thickens slightly.

3 Add chicken and pepper; stir until heated through. Stir in green onion just before serving.

4 Divide pastry puff bases among serving plates; top with chicken mixture then puff pastry tops.

SERVES 4

per serving 42.8g fat; 2470kJ

tip If you have leftover cooked peas, add them to the chicken mixture.
serving suggestion Serve with steamed vegetables.

Score the top of each pastry square in a crosshatch pattern

thai chicken salad

Palm sugar, made from the distilled sap of the sugar palm, is also known as jaggery or gula jawa and is available from Asian speciality shops. You need to purchase a large barbecued chicken weighing approximately 900g for this recipe.

350g yellow string beans, trimmed, halved
1 teaspoon finely grated lime rind
2 tablespoons lime juice
1 tablespoon grated palm sugar
1 clove garlic, crushed
1 tablespoon peanut oil
1/2 cup loosely packed, finely chopped fresh mint
2 teaspoons sweet chilli sauce
1 tablespoon fish sauce
4 cups (400g) shredded chicken
1 cup loosely packed, coarsely chopped fresh coriander
250g cherry tomatoes, halved
1 red thai chilli, chopped finely

1 Boil, steam or microwave beans until almost tender. Rinse under cold water; drain.

2 Meanwhile, combine rind, juice, sugar, garlic, oil, mint and sauces in large bowl. Add beans, chicken, three quarters of the coriander and tomato; toss gently to combine.

3 Top salad with remaining coriander and chilli just before serving.

SERVES 4

per serving 13.6g fat; 1136kJ

tip Chopped snake beans can be substituted for the yellow string bean.

serving suggestion Salad can also be served in lettuce or cabbage leaves.

roasted capsicum, fetta and walnut salad

PREPARATION TIME 10 MINUTES • COOKING TIME 5 MINUTES

You need to purchase a large barbecued chicken weighing approximately 900g for this recipe.

**300g quick-cook pasta
frilled shells
270g jar char-grilled
capsicum in oil
150g fetta cheese,
chopped coarsely
3 cups (400g) coarsely
chopped chicken
1/3 cup (35g) toasted walnuts,
chopped coarsely
1 cup loosely packed fresh
basil leaves
1/4 cup (60ml) red wine vinegar
1 clove garlic, crushed
2 teaspoons seeded mustard**

1 Cook pasta in large saucepan of boiling water, uncovered, until just tender; drain. Rinse under cold running water; drain.

2 Meanwhile, drain capsicum. Reserve 1/3 cup of the capsicum oil; chop capsicum coarsely. Combine capsicum and pasta in large bowl with cheese, chicken, walnuts and basil.

3 Combine reserved oil with vinegar, garlic and mustard in screw-top jar; shake well. Drizzle dressing over chicken mixture; toss gently to combine.

SERVES 4

per serving 22.2g fat; 2301kJ
tips Goat cheese or any soft, crumbly cheese can be used instead of the fetta.
Toasted pecan halves make a nice change from walnuts.

baked pasta and chicken carbonara

PREPARATION TIME 10 MINUTES • COOKING TIME 20 MINUTES

You need to purchase a large barbecued chicken weighing approximately 900g for this recipe.

250g spaghetti
1 tablespoon olive oil
500g button mushrooms,
  quartered
2 cloves garlic, crushed
1 teaspoon coarsely
  chopped fresh thyme
¼ cup (60ml) dry white wine
¾ cup (180ml) chicken stock
425g jar carbonara sauce
3 green onions, sliced thickly
4 cups (400g) shredded chicken
⅔ cup (50g) finely grated
  parmesan cheese
⅓ cup (25g) stale breadcrumbs

1 Cook pasta in large saucepan of boiling water, uncovered, until just tender; drain. Rinse under cold running water; drain.

2 Meanwhile, preheat oven to very hot. Heat oil in large frying pan; cook mushrooms, garlic and thyme, stirring, until mushrooms are lightly browned. Add wine and stock; bring to a boil. Cook, stirring, about 5 minutes or until liquid is reduced by half; remove from heat.

3 Add pasta to mushroom mixture with sauce, onion, chicken and half of the cheese; toss gently to combine.

4 Combine remaining cheese and breadcrumbs in small bowl. Pour pasta mixture into lightly greased 3-litre (12-cup) baking dish; sprinkle top with breadcrumb mixture. Bake, uncovered, in very hot oven, about 10 minutes or until top is lightly browned.

SERVES 4

per serving 30g fat; 2914kJ

chicken tostadas

Refried beans are sold, canned, in most supermarkets, along with cryovac-packed flour tortillas. Made of pinto beans that are just parboiled then fried with various seasonings, refried beans are also known by their Mexican name of frijoles refritos. You need to purchase one small iceberg lettuce as well as a large barbecued chicken weighing approximately 900g for this recipe.

4 large flour tortillas
1/2 cup (120g) canned refried beans
1/2 cup (130g) medium chunky salsa
3 cups (400g) coarsely chopped chicken
11/2 cups (125g) grated cheddar cheese
4 cups (240g) finely shredded iceberg lettuce
2 medium tomatoes (380g), chopped coarsely
3 green onions, sliced thinly
1/2 cup (120g) light sour cream

1 Preheat grill to hot. Place tortillas, in single layer, on oven trays.

2 Combine beans and salsa in small bowl. Divide bean mixture among tortillas; top with chicken and cheese. Place under preheated grill until cheese melts and tortillas' edges crisp.

3 Top tostadas with lettuce, tomato, onion and sour cream to serve.

SERVES 4

per serving 24.5g fat; 1902kJ

tip Store uncooked tortillas, sealed tightly, in the refrigerator or freezer.

Place tortillas on oven tray before topping

chicken laksa

PREPARATION TIME 10 MINUTES • COOKING TIME 5 MINUTES

This spicy Malaysian soup has become so popular that its name has made its way into our everyday language. You need to purchase a large barbecued chicken weighing approximately 900g for this recipe.

250g fresh egg noodles
1 teaspoon peanut oil
$^1/_4$ cup (75g) laksa paste
$3^1/_4$ cups (800ml) light coconut milk
1 litre (4 cups) chicken stock
2 tablespoons lime juice
1 tablespoon sugar
1 tablespoon fish sauce
6 kaffir lime leaves, torn
3 cups (400g) coarsely chopped chicken
1 cup (80g) bean sprouts
$^1/_2$ cup loosely packed fresh vietnamese mint leaves

1 Rinse noodles in strainer under hot running water. Separate noodles with fork; drain.

2 Meanwhile, heat oil in large saucepan; cook paste, stirring, until fragrant. Stir in coconut milk, stock, juice, sugar, sauce and lime leaves; bring to a boil. Reduce heat; simmer, covered, 3 minutes. Add chicken; stir until laksa is heated through.

3 Divide noodles among serving bowls. Ladle laksa over noodles; top with sprouts and mint.

SERVES 4

per serving 29.3g fat; 2486kJ

tip You can substitute your favourite kind of noodle for the egg noodles.

creamy pesto chicken with gnocchi

PREPARATION TIME 10 MINUTES • COOKING TIME 5 MINUTES

Gnocchi, small Italian "dumplings" usually made from mashed potato or semolina, can be boiled, baked or fried. You need to purchase a large barbecued chicken weighing approximately 900g for this recipe.

500g fresh gnocchi
1 tablespoon olive oil
2 cloves garlic, crushed
1/2 cup (125ml) dry white wine
1/4 cup (60g) basil pesto
300ml cream
3 cups (400g) coarsely
    chopped chicken
2 tablespoons fresh basil leaves

1 Cook gnocchi in large saucepan of boiling water, uncovered, about 5 minutes or until gnocchi rise to the surface and are just tender; drain.

2 Meanwhile, heat oil in large saucepan; cook garlic, stirring, until fragrant. Add wine, pesto and cream; bring to a boil. Reduce heat; simmer, uncovered, 3 minutes. Add chicken and gnocchi; stir until heated through. Top with fresh basil to serve.

SERVES 4

per serving 49.5g fat; 2983kJ

tip This recipe is best made close to serving time.

chicken and vegie pie with fillo top

PREPARATION TIME 20 MINUTES • COOKING TIME 10 MINUTES

We used frozen fillo pastry sheets, available in 375g packets from your supermarket. You need to purchase a large barbecued chicken weighing approximately 900g for this recipe.

Layer fillo pastry over dish

Roll edge of pastry

60g butter
1 medium leek (350g), sliced thinly
1/3 cup (50g) plain flour
3/4 cup (180ml) milk
1 cup (250ml) chicken stock
4 cups (400g) shredded chicken
2 1/2 cups (350g) frozen peas, corn and capsicum mix
1/4 cup loosely packed, coarsely chopped fresh flat-leaf parsley
4 sheets fillo pastry
cooking-oil spray

1 Preheat oven to hot.

2 Melt butter in large saucepan; cook leek, stirring, until softened. Add flour; cook, stirring, until mixture bubbles and thickens. Gradually stir in milk and stock; heat, stirring, until mixture boils and thickens. Add chicken, vegetables and parsley; stir until heated through.

3 Spoon chicken pie filling into shallow 1.5-litre (6-cup) ovenproof dish. Place one sheet of pastry over filling; spray with cooking-oil spray. Repeat process with remaining pastry, overlapping pastry around dish. Roll and fold pastry around edge of dish. Spray top of pastry with cooking-oil spray. Bake, uncovered, in hot oven 10 minutes.

SERVES 4

per serving 25.3g fat; 2037kJ
tip Pie filling can be made a day ahead.
serving suggestion Serve with a crisp garden salad.

thai-style pumpkin soup

PREPARATION TIME 10 MINUTES • COOKING TIME 5 MINUTES

You need to purchase a large barbecued chicken weighing approximately 900g for this recipe.

¹/₄ cup (75g) red curry paste
2 x 420g cans cream of
pumpkin soup
3¹/₄ cups (800ml) light
coconut milk
1¹/₂ cups (375ml)
chicken stock
3 cups (400g) coarsely
chopped chicken
4 green onions, sliced thinly
¹/₄ cup loosely packed, coarsely
chopped fresh basil

1 Cook curry paste, stirring, in large heated saucepan until fragrant. Add soup, coconut milk and stock; bring to a boil.

2 Add chicken; reduce heat. Simmer, stirring, until soup is heated through. Stir in onion and basil just before serving.

SERVES 4

per serving 23.7g fat; 1498kJ

tip You can adjust the amount of curry paste to suit your taste.

serving suggestion Herb scones make a great accompaniment with this soup.

chicken with cacciatore-style sauce

PREPARATION TIME 15 MINUTES • COOKING TIME 10 MINUTES

Quarter barbecued chicken

Skin quartered pieces of barbecued chicken

1 tablespoon olive oil
1 medium brown onion (150g), chopped finely
2 cloves garlic, crushed
1 tablespoon tomato paste
2 x 400g cans tomatoes
1/2 cup (125ml) dry red wine
2 bay leaves
4 anchovy fillets, drained, chopped finely
1 cup (120g) seeded kalamata olives
2 tablespoons fresh oregano leaves
1 large (900g) barbecued chicken, quartered, skinned

1 Heat oil in large saucepan; cook onion and garlic, stirring, until onion softens. Add paste, undrained crushed tomatoes, wine, bay leaves, anchovy and olives; bring to a boil. Reduce heat; simmer, uncovered, 4 minutes. Discard bay leaves; stir oregano through sauce.

2 Add chicken to sauce; stir until heated through.

SERVES 4

per serving 16.1g fat; 1549kJ

serving suggestion Serve with a bowl of freshly cooked short pasta, such as farfalle or penne.

chicken, basil and cabbage salad

You need to purchase a medium chinese cabbage as well as a large barbecued chicken weighing approximately 900g for this recipe.

4 cups (400g) shredded chicken
4 cups (320g) finely shredded chinese cabbage
4 green onions, sliced thinly
1/4 cup firmly packed, finely chopped fresh basil
2 cloves garlic, crushed
1/4 cup (60ml) peanut oil
1/4 cup (60ml) lime juice
2 tablespoons fish sauce
1 tablespoon sugar

1 Place chicken, cabbage, onion and basil in large bowl.

2 Combine garlic, oil, juice, fish sauce and sugar in screw-top jar; shake well. Drizzle dressing over salad; toss gently to combine.

SERVES 4

per serving 22.4g fat; 1410kJ

moroccan chicken salad with couscous

PREPARATION TIME 10 MINUTES • COOKING TIME 5 MINUTES

You need to purchase a large barbecued chicken weighing approximately 900g for this recipe.

1 cup (250ml) vegetable stock
1¹/2 cups (300g) couscous
1 medium red onion (170g), sliced thinly
4 cups (400g) shredded chicken
¹/2 cup (75g) coarsely chopped dried apricots
¹/2 cup (80g) sultanas
¹/4 cup loosely packed, finely chopped fresh mint
1 tablespoon pine nuts
2 teaspoons cumin seeds
³/4 cup (180ml) fat-free french dressing

1 Bring stock to a boil in large saucepan; remove from heat. Stir in couscous. Cover; stand about 5 minutes or until stock is absorbed, fluffing with fork. Stir in onion, chicken, apricot, sultanas and mint.

2 Meanwhile, stir pine nuts and seeds in small frying pan over low heat until just fragrant. Add to couscous with dressing; toss gently to combine.

SERVES 4

per serving 12.1g fat; 2670kJ

chicken and lime noodle salad

Bean-thread noodles or vermicelli are also known as cellophane or glass noodles. You need to purchase a large barbecued chicken weighing approximately 900g for this recipe.

250g bean-thread noodles
1 medium carrot (120g)
1 lebanese cucumber (130g), halved, seeded
2 green onions, sliced thinly
1 medium red capsicum (200g), sliced thinly
4 cups (400g) shredded chicken
1/2 cup loosely packed fresh vietnamese mint leaves
1/2 cup loosely packed fresh coriander leaves
3 red thai chillies, seeded, sliced thinly
2 cloves garlic, crushed
1/3 cup (80ml) lime juice
1/3 cup (80ml) peanut oil
2 tablespoons fish sauce
1 tablespoon sugar

1 Place noodles in large heatproof bowl; cover with boiling water. Stand until tender; drain.

2 Meanwhile, using vegetable peeler, slice carrot and cucumber into ribbons.

3 Combine noodles, carrot and cucumber in large bowl with onion, capsicum, chicken, mint, coriander, chilli and combined remaining ingredients; toss gently to combine.

SERVES 4

per serving 27.0g fat; 2308kJ

tips For an even more refreshing salad, refrigerate the drained noodles overnight before combining with remaining ingredients.

Substitute regular mint or add extra coriander if you can't find vietnamese mint.

serving suggestion Serve accompanied with small bowls of extra coriander leaves and finely sliced red thai chillies.

vietnamese chicken salad

PREPARATION TIME 20 MINUTES • COOKING TIME 5 MINUTES

This dish, known as ga xe phai, is one of Vietnam's most popular salads. You need to purchase one small chinese cabbage as well as a large barbecued chicken weighing approximately 900g for this recipe.

100g snow peas, trimmed
4 cups (400g) shredded chicken
4 cups (320g) finely shredded chinese cabbage
4 garlic chives, chopped finely
1 medium red onion (170g), sliced thinly
1/2 cup loosely packed, coarsely chopped fresh mint
1 teaspoon sambal oelek
1 tablespoon sesame oil
1/3 cup (80ml) lime juice
1/3 cup (80ml) fish sauce
2 teaspoons sugar
1/2 cup loosely packed fresh coriander leaves

1 Place snow peas in medium bowl. Cover with boiling water; drain immediately. Cover snow peas with cold water in same bowl; stand 2 minutes. Drain; slice thinly.

2 Combine snow peas in large bowl with chicken, cabbage, chives, onion and mint.

3 Combine sambal oelek, oil, juice, sauce and sugar in screw-top jar; shake well. Drizzle salad with chilli lime dressing; toss gently to combine then sprinkle coriander over salad.

SERVES 4

per serving 13.6g fat; 1159kJ
serving suggestion Serve with puffed prawn crackers.

chicken caesar salad

PREPARATION TIME 20 MINUTES

Caesar salad is said to have been created in the 1920s by Caesar Cardini at his restaurant in Tijuana, Mexico. You need to purchase a large barbecued chicken weighing approximately 900g for this recipe.

100g parmesan cheese
1 egg
1 clove garlic, quartered
2 tablespoons lemon juice
1/2 teaspoon dijon mustard
10 anchovy fillets, drained
3/4 cup (180ml) olive oil
1 large cos lettuce, torn
3 cups (400g) coarsely
 chopped chicken
170g packet toasted croutons

1 Using vegetable peeler, slice cheese into ribbons.

2 Blend or process egg, garlic, juice, mustard and half of the anchovy until smooth. With motor operating, add oil in thin, steady stream; process until dressing just thickens.

3 Just before serving, combine cheese in large bowl with lettuce, chicken, croutons and remaining anchovy; toss gently to combine. Drizzle with anchovy dressing.

SERVES 4

per serving 72.8g fat; 3600kJ
tips Dressing can be made a day ahead and refrigerated, covered.
You can grate the parmesan rather than shave it, and mix it in with the dressing.

chicken, witlof and cashew salad

PREPARATION TIME 20 MINUTES

Like mushrooms, witlof is grown in the dark to retain its pale colour and bittersweet taste. Sometimes spelled witloof, and in some places known as belgian endive or chicory, this versatile vegetable is as good eaten cooked as it is raw. You need to purchase a large barbecued chicken weighing approximately 900g for this recipe.

1 medium witlof (175g)
2 baby cos lettuces
1 medium yellow capsicum (200g), sliced thinly
1 small red onion (100g), sliced thinly
1 cup (150g) roasted unsalted cashews
4 cups (400g) shredded chicken

DRESSING
1 cup (280g) yogurt
2 cloves garlic, crushed
2 teaspoons finely grated lemon rind
1/4 cup (60ml) lemon juice
1/4 cup loosely packed, coarsely chopped fresh coriander

1 Trim and discard 1cm from witlof base; separate leaves. Trim core from lettuce; separate leaves.

2 Place witlof and lettuce in large bowl with capsicum, onion, cashews, chicken and dressing; toss gently to combine.

dressing Combine ingredients in screw-top jar; shake well.

SERVES 4

per serving 26.3g fat; 1737kJ

tips Witlof is also delicious braised, grilled or baked. Witlof is particularly compatible with asparagus, ham and various dairy products such as cream or fresh cheeses.

Roast cashews briefly in a small dry heavy-based frying pan, stirring, over medium heat to bring out their flavour.

greek chicken salad

PREPARATION TIME 15 MINUTES • COOKING TIME 15 MINUTES

You need to purchase a large barbecued chicken weighing approximately 900g for this recipe.

375g small shell pasta
1/4 cup loosely packed, coarsely
chopped fresh oregano
1/2 cup (125ml) olive oil
1/4 cup (60ml) lemon juice
4 cups (400g) shredded chicken
1 medium red onion (170g),
sliced thinly
500g cherry tomatoes, quartered
2 lebanese cucumbers (260g),
chopped coarsely
1 large green capsicum (350g),
chopped coarsely
1 cup (120g) seeded
kalamata olives
280g jar marinated
artichoke hearts, drained,
chopped coarsely
200g fetta cheese,
chopped coarsely

1 Cook pasta in large saucepan of boiling water, uncovered, until just tender; drain. Rinse under cold water; drain.

2 Meanwhile, place 2 tablespoons of the oregano, oil and juice in screw-top jar; shake well.

3 Place pasta in large bowl with chicken, onion, tomato, cucumber, capsicum, olives, artichoke, fetta and dressing; toss gently to combine. Top salad with remaining oregano.

SERVES 4

per serving 49.3g fat; 3852kJ

tips You can use your favourite kind of pasta for this recipe.

Use the oil from the artichokes to make the dressing if you wish.

tangy chicken salad

PREPARATION TIME 20 MINUTES

You need to purchase one small chinese cabbage as well as a large barbecued chicken weighing approximately 900g for this recipe.

1 medium carrot (120g)
1 telegraph cucumber (400g)
4 cups (400g) shredded chicken
4 cups (320g) finely shredded chinese cabbage
2¹/₂ cups (200g) bean sprouts
3 green onions, sliced thinly
3 small red radishes, sliced thinly
¹/₄ cup (35g) roasted unsalted peanuts, chopped coarsely

DRESSING
¹/₄ cup (60ml) fish sauce
¹/₄ cup (60ml) lime juice
1 tablespoon rice vinegar
1 tablespoon sugar
1 tablespoon sesame oil
1 clove garlic, crushed
¹/₂ teaspoon sambal oelek

1 Using vegetable peeler, slice carrot and cucumber into ribbons. Place carrot and cucumber in large bowl with chicken, cabbage, sprouts, onion and radish.

2 Drizzle salad with dressing; toss gently to combine. Top with peanuts just before serving.

dressing Combine ingredients in screw-top jar; shake until sugar dissolves.

SERVES 4

per serving 17.7g fat; 1407kJ

tip You can prepare the salad several hours ahead. Add the dressing just before serving.

Cut whole chicken in half lengthways then in half again through centre

Separate breasts from wings and thighs from legs

Halve wings and cut remaining pieces into thirds

spicy barbecued chicken and bok choy

PREPARATION TIME 10 MINUTES • COOKING TIME 10 MINUTES

This recipe shows how to cut a barbecued chicken in the Chinese manner, for those times when you want pieces rather than chopped chicken.

2 cups (400g) long-grain white rice
1 large (900g) barbecued chicken
1/2 cup (125ml) chicken stock
1/3 cup (80ml) dry red wine
1/3 cup (80ml) tomato sauce
1 tablespoon oyster sauce
1 tablespoon rice vinegar
1/2 teaspoon five-spice powder
250g baby bok choy, sliced thinly

1 Cook rice in large saucepan of boiling water, uncovered, until just tender; drain.

2 Meanwhile, using sharp knife, halve chicken lengthways. Cut both halves crossways through the centre. Cut to separate breasts from wings and thighs from legs. You will have eight pieces. Cut each wing in half; cut all other pieces into thirds.

3 Heat wok or large frying pan. Add stock, wine, sauces, vinegar and five-spice; stir until mixture comes to a boil.

4 Add chicken and bok choy. Reduce heat; simmer, uncovered, until chicken is heated through. Serve chicken mixture on rice.

SERVES 4

per serving 20.4g fat; 2850kJ

chicken with almonds and date sauce

PREPARATION TIME 10 MINUTES • COOKING TIME 15 MINUTES

1 tablespoon olive oil
1 large brown onion (200g),
  halved, sliced thinly
1¹/₂ teaspoons ground cinnamon
2 teaspoons finely grated
  orange rind
¹/₄ teaspoon cayenne pepper
1¹/₂ cups (375ml) chicken stock
¹/₂ cup (85g) seeded dates,
  chopped coarsely
1 large (900g) barbecued
  chicken, quartered
1 cup (250ml) orange juice
1 cup (250ml) water
2 cups (400g) couscous
20g butter
¹/₄ cup (35g) toasted
  slivered almonds

1 Heat oil in large frying pan;
  cook onion, stirring, until lightly
  browned. Add cinnamon, rind,
  cayenne and stock; bring to a
  boil. Reduce heat; simmer,
  uncovered, 4 minutes. Add dates
  and chicken; stir until mixture is
  heated through.

2 Meanwhile, combine juice and
  the water in large saucepan;
  bring to a boil. Remove from
  heat; add couscous. Cover; stand
  about 5 minutes or until water is
  absorbed, fluffing with fork
  occasionally. Stir in butter.

3 Serve chicken mixture sprinkled
  with almonds on couscous.

SERVES 4

per serving 34.1g fat; 3715kJ
tips Hot, pungent cayenne is also
sometimes just called red pepper.
You can substitute sultanas for
the dates.

chicken with olives and lemon

PREPARATION TIME 20 MINUTES • COOKING TIME 10 MINUTES

Harissa is a North African spice paste used as a meat rub or condiment. If you can't find it, use chilli paste or hot pepper sauce. You need to purchase a large barbecued chicken weighing approximately 900g for this recipe.

1/4 cup (60ml) olive oil
1 medium red onion (170g),
   sliced thickly
3 cloves garlic, crushed
6 medium egg tomatoes
   (450g), chopped coarsely
300g can white beans,
   rinsed, drained
4 cups (400g) shredded chicken
1/2 cup (60g) seeded
   kalamata olives
1/4 cup firmly packed fresh
   basil leaves
2 tablespoons coarsely chopped
   fresh flat-leaf parsley
2 tablespoons red wine vinegar
1/2 teaspoon sugar
2 teaspoons finely grated
   lemon rind
1/2 teaspoon harissa

1 Heat 1 tablespoon of the oil in large wok or frying pan; stir-fry onion and garlic until onion softens. Add tomato; cook, stirring, 3 minutes.

2 Add beans, chicken and olives; stir-fry until heated through. Add remaining oil, basil, parsley, vinegar, sugar, rind and harissa; stir-fry until just hot.

SERVES 4

per serving 19.4g fat; 1231kJ
serving suggestion This recipe is best served with couscous.

thai chicken in lettuce-leaf cups

PREPARATION TIME 20 MINUTES

You need to purchase a large barbecued chicken weighing approximately 900g for this recipe.

8 large iceberg lettuce leaves
1 tablespoon kecap manis
1 tablespoon sesame oil
1 tablespoon lime juice
1 large zucchini (150g), grated coarsely
1 medium carrot (120g), grated coarsely
2 green onions, sliced thinly
1 medium red capsicum (200g), sliced thinly
4 cups (400g) shredded chicken
1 tablespoon finely chopped fresh mint
2 tablespoons coarsely chopped fresh coriander
2 tablespoons sweet chilli sauce

1 Trim lettuce-leaf edges with scissors. Place leaves in large bowl of iced water; refrigerate.

2 Meanwhile, combine kecap manis, oil and juice in large bowl. Add zucchini, carrot, onion, capsicum, chicken, mint and half of the coriander; toss gently to combine.

3 Dry lettuce; divide leaves among serving plates. Top with chicken mixture; drizzle with combined sauce and remaining coriander.

SERVES 4

per serving 13.7g fat; 1087kJ

tip If you can't find kecap manis, substitute it with 1 tablespoon dark soy sauce and 1 tablespoon brown sugar, simmered together in a small saucepan until the sugar has dissolved. Cool before using.

chicken with creamy sun-dried tomato sauce

PREPARATION TIME 10 MINUTES • COOKING TIME 15 MINUTES

1 tablespoon olive oil
1 medium brown onion (150g),
  chopped finely
2 teaspoons tomato paste
2/3 cup (100g) drained sun-dried
  tomatoes, chopped coarsely
1/4 cup (60ml) dry white wine
1/2 cup (125ml) chicken stock
300ml cream
2 tablespoons coarsely chopped
  fresh sage
1 large (900g) barbecued
  chicken, skinned, quartered

1 Heat oil in large frying pan;
  cook onion, stirring, until onion
  is lightly browned.

2 Add paste, tomato and wine;
  cook, uncovered, until liquid is
  almost evaporated. Add stock,
  cream and sage; bring to a boil.
  Add chicken; reduce heat.
  Simmer, uncovered, until sauce
  thickens slightly and mixture is
  heated through.

SERVES 4

per serving 17.0g fat; 1462kJ
tip Sage can be substituted with
any other fresh herb.
serving suggestion Serve with
steamed white rice.

chicken turnovers

PREPARATION TIME 10 MINUTES • COOKING TIME 20 MINUTES

In this recipe, we used a frozen vegetable mix containing peas, carrots and cauliflower, although any frozen vegetables of equivalent weight would work just as well. You need to purchase a large barbecued chicken weighing approximately 900g for this recipe.

4 cups (400g) shredded chicken
310g can creamed corn
³/₄ cup (90g) coarsely grated cheddar cheese
2 cups (280g) frozen vegetable mix, thawed
¹/₄ cup (60ml) cream
3 sheets ready-rolled puff pastry
1 egg, beaten lightly

1 Preheat oven to moderate.

2 Combine chicken, corn, cheese, vegetables and cream in large bowl; mix well.

3 Cut each pastry sheet into four squares. Place 2 heaped tablespoons of filling on each square; brush around edges with cold water. Fold pastry over diagonally to form triangle; pinch edges together to seal. Place on lightly greased oven tray; brush with egg. Repeat with remaining pastry.

4 Bake, uncovered, in moderate oven about 20 minutes or until turnovers are lightly browned.

MAKES 12

per serving 16.6g fat; 1153kJ

tip Uncooked turnovers can be frozen, covered tightly, until required.

tom kha gai

This Thai chicken soup is one of our favourites. You need to purchase a large barbecued chicken weighing approximately 900g for this recipe.

2 teaspoons peanut oil
1 tablespoon finely chopped fresh lemon grass
3 teaspoons grated fresh ginger
1 clove garlic, crushed
3 green thai chillies, chopped finely
4 kaffir lime leaves, sliced thinly
1/4 teaspoon ground turmeric
31/4 cups (800ml) light coconut milk
3 cups (750ml) chicken stock
2 cups (500ml) water
1 tablespoon fish sauce
4 cups (400g) shredded chicken
3 green onions, sliced thinly
1/4 cup (60ml) lime juice
2 tablespoons coarsely chopped fresh coriander

1 Heat oil in large saucepan; cook lemon grass, ginger, garlic, chilli, lime leaves and turmeric, stirring, about 2 minutes or until fragrant.

2 Stir in coconut milk, stock, the water and sauce; bring to a boil. Add chicken; reduce heat. Simmer, uncovered, 10 minutes.

3 Just before serving, stir in onion, juice and coriander.

SERVES 4

per serving 23.7g fat; 1498kJ
serving suggestion Top with fresh mint and bean sprouts, if desired.

sesame chicken salad

PREPARATION TIME 15 MINUTES

You need to purchase a large barbecued chicken weighing approximately 900g for this recipe.

150g snow peas
4 cups (400g) shredded chicken
100g snow pea sprouts
2 cups (160g) bean sprouts
2 trimmed sticks celery (150g),
  sliced thinly
4 green onions, sliced thinly
1 tablespoon roasted
  sesame seeds

DRESSING
2 tablespoons peanut oil
2 teaspoons sesame oil
1/2 teaspoon five-spice powder
2 tablespoons kecap manis
1 tablespoon lime juice

1 Place snow peas in medium bowl. Cover with boiling water; drain immediately. Cover snow peas with cold water in same bowl; stand 2 minutes. Drain; slice thinly.

2 Combine snow peas in large bowl with chicken, snow pea sprouts, bean sprouts, celery, onion and dressing; toss gently to combine. Sprinkle with sesame seeds to serve.

dressing Combine ingredients in screw-top jar; shake well.

SERVES 4

per serving 18.4g fat; 1188kJ
tip Sugar snap peas can also be used in this recipe.

chicken nachos

PREPARATION TIME 15 MINUTES • COOKING TIME 10 MINUTES

*Pizza cheese, a convenient blend of grated processed cheddar, mozzarella
and parmesan cheeses, is great for nachos, tacos and pizza. You need to purchase a large
barbecued chicken weighing approximately 900g for this recipe.*

1 tablespoon vegetable oil
1 medium brown onion (150g),
    chopped finely
425g can mexican-style
    beans, drained
4 cups (400g) shredded chicken
390g jar mild nachos
    topping sauce
230g packet corn chips
2 cups (220g) grated
    pizza cheese
1 medium avocado (250g),
    mashed coarsely
2/3 cup (160g) sour cream

1 Heat oil in medium frying pan;
   cook onion, stirring, until
   softened. Stir in beans, chicken
   and sauce; bring to a boil.
   Reduce heat; simmer, uncovered,
   about 3 minutes or until mixture
   thickens slightly.

2 Meanwhile, divide corn chips
   among four microwave-safe
   serving dishes; top each with
   cheese. Microwave, one plate at
   a time, uncovered, on HIGH
   about 1 minute or until cheese
   has melted.

3 Top plates of corn chips and
   cheese with equal amounts of
   chicken mixture, avocado and
   sour cream.

SERVES 4

per serving 65g fat; 3997kJ

chicken pho

PREPARATION TIME 15 MINUTES • COOKING TIME 15 MINUTES

Large bowls of pho are a breakfast favourite throughout Vietnam, but we like to eat it any time of day. Dried rice noodles are often labelled rice stick noodles. You need to purchase a large barbecued chicken weighing approximately 900g for this recipe.

1.5 litres (6 cups) chicken stock
2 teaspoons grated fresh ginger
1 clove garlic, crushed
1/4 cup (60ml) fish sauce
1 tablespoon finely chopped
   fresh lemon grass
1 teaspoon sambal oelek
4 green onions, sliced thinly
100g dried rice noodles
4 cups (400g) shredded chicken
1 cup (80g) bean sprouts
1/2 cup firmly packed fresh
   mint leaves
2 tablespoons finely chopped
   fresh coriander

1 Combine stock, ginger, garlic, sauce and lemon grass in large saucepan; bring to a boil. Reduce heat; simmer, covered, 8 minutes. Remove from heat; stir in sambal oelek and onion.

2 Meanwhile, place noodles in medium heatproof bowl; cover with boiling water. Stand until just tender; drain.

3 Divide noodles among serving bowls; top with chicken. Ladle soup over chicken; top with sprouts, mint and coriander.

SERVES 4

per serving 7.2g fat; 1013kJ

tip If noodles become cold, reheat them by pouring boiling water over them while still in the colander.

chicken cuts

LARGE BARBECUED CHICKEN

BARBECUED CHICKEN MEAT,
coarsely chopped

BARBECUED CHICKEN MEAT,
shredded

BREAST FILLET
skinned and boned half breast

THIGH FILLET
skinned and boned thigh

TENDERLOIN
thin strip of meat lying just under the breast

DRUMSTICK
leg with skin and bone intact

LARGE WING
weighs more than 125g

THIGH
skin and bone intact

DRUMETTE
wing trimmed to resemble drumstick

WING
weighs less than 125g

chicken cuts   115

glossary

angel hair pasta small, circular nests of very fine, delicate pasta.

antipasto We used a bottled combination of assorted roasted vegetables.

artichoke hearts centre of the globe artichoke; sold in cans, or loose in brine.

bamboo shoots the shoots of bamboo plants, available in cans.

barbecue sauce a spicy, tomato-based sauce.

bean sprouts also known as bean shoots; tender new growths of assorted beans and seeds germinated for consumption as sprouts.

beans

BUTTER another name for lima beans; a large off-white bean with a mealy texture and sweet flavour.

MEXICAN-STYLE a canned mixture of kidney, haricot or pinto beans cooked with tomato, peppers, onion, garlic and various spices.

KIDNEY medium-sized red bean, slightly floury yet sweet in flavour.

REFRIED pinto beans cooked twice; soaked and boiled then mashed and fried, traditionally in lard.

YELLOW STRING also known as wax, french, butter and runner beans; basically yellow-coloured fresh "green" beans.

beetroot also known as red beets or simply, beets; firm, round deep purple-red root vegetable having a sweet distinctive taste and a refined smooth texture.

black bean sauce a Chinese sauce made from fermented soy beans, spices, water and wheat flour.

bok choy also called pak choi or chinese white cabbage; has a fresh, mild mustard taste and is good braised or in stir-fries. Baby bok choy is also available and is slightly more tender than bok choy.

breadcrumbs

PACKAGED fine-textured, crunchy, purchased, white breadcrumbs.

STALE 1- or 2-day-old bread made into crumbs by grating, blending or processing.

burghul also known as bulghur wheat; hulled steamed wheat kernels that, once dried, are crushed into various size grains.

butter use salted or unsalted ("sweet") butter; 125g is equal to 1 stick butter.

carbonara sauce an Italian pasta sauce traditionally made from pancetta, cream, cheese and egg. We used a bottled version which can be found in supermarkets.

cayenne pepper a thin-fleshed, long, extremely hot red chilli; usually purchased dried and ground.

cheese

CHEDDAR the most common cow milk "tasty" cheese; should be aged, hard and have a pronounced bite.

FETTA Greek in origin; a crumbly textured goat or sheep milk cheese with a sharp, salty taste.

HALOUMI a firm, creamed coloured sheep milk cheese matured in brine; somewhat like a minty, salty fetta in flavour.

MOZZARELLA a semi-soft cheese with a delicate, fresh taste; traditionally made from buffalo milk.

PARMESAN a sharp-tasting, dry, hard cheese, made from skim or part-skim milk and aged for at least a year before being sold.

PIZZA a commercial blend of processed grated cheddar, mozzarella and parmesan.

chermoulla a piquant Moroccan paste mixture of fresh and ground spices including coriander, cumin and paprika.

chickpeas also called garbanzos, hummus or channa; an irregularly round, sandy-coloured legume.

chillies available in many different types and sizes, both fresh and dried. Generally the smaller the chilli, the hotter it is; removing seeds and membranes lessens the heat level. Use rubber gloves when seeding and chopping chillies as they can burn your skin.

DRIED CRUSHED sold in flake form.

JALAPEÑO sold finely chopped or whole, bottled in vinegar, as well as fresh.

POWDER made from ground chillies; substitute ½ teaspoon chilli powder for 1 medium chopped fresh chilli.

RED THAI small, medium-hot, and bright red in colour.

SAUCE we use a hot Chinese variety made of chillies, salt and vinegar; use sparingly, increasing amounts to taste.

SWEET CHILLI SAUCE comparatively mild, Thai-type sauce made from red chillies, sugar, garlic and white wine vinegar.

chinese broccoli also known as gai larn.

chinese cabbage also known as peking cabbage or wong bok.

choy sum also known as flowering bok choy or flowering white cabbage.

coconut

CREAM made from coconut and water.

MILK pure, unsweetened coconut milk; a lower-fat type is also sold.

coriander also known as cilantro or chinese parsley; bright-green-leafed herb with a pungent flavour. Also sold as seeds or ground.

corn flake crumbs a packaged product of crushed corn flakes.

cornflour also known as cornstarch; used as a thickening agent in cooking.

cos lettuce also known as romaine lettuce; the traditional caesar salad lettuce.

couscous a fine, grain-like cereal product, originally from North Africa; made from semolina.

cream

FRESH (minimum fat content 35%) also known as pure cream and pouring cream; contains no additives.

LIGHT SOUR (minimum fat content 18%) cream specifically cultured to produce its characteristic tart flavour; thinner than normal sour cream.

croutons cubes of bread that have been browned by baking or frying.

cucumber

LEBANESE short, slender and thin-skinned; also known as the european or burpless cucumber.

TELEGRAPH long and green with ridges running down its entire length; also known as continental cucumber.

curly endive also known as frisée; a loosely headed green vegetable having curly, ragged edged leaves and a slightly bitter flavour.

curry paste

GREEN consists of red onion, green chilli, soy bean oil, garlic, lemon grass, galangal, shrimp paste, citrus peel and coriander seeds.

MADRAS consists of coriander, cumin, pepper, turmeric, chilli, garlic, ginger, vinegar and oil.

RED consists of red chilli, onion, garlic, soy bean oil, lemon rind, shrimp paste, cumin, paprika, turmeric and pepper.

TANDOORI consists of garlic, tamarind, coriander, ginger, chilli and spices.

TIKKA consists of chilli, coriander, cumin, lentil flour, garlic, ginger, oil, turmeric, fennel, pepper, cloves, cinnamon and cardamom.

VINDALOO a fiery hot/sour flavour; consists of coriander, cumin, turmeric, chilli, ginger, garlic, tamarind, lentil flour and spices.

curry powder a blend of ground spices; can include: dried chilli, cinnamon, coriander, cumin, fennel, fenugreek, mace, cardamom and turmeric.

eggplant purple-skinned vegetable also known as aubergine.

fillo pastry also known as phyllo; tissue-thin pastry sheets purchased chilled or frozen.

fish sauce also called nam pla or nuoc nam; made from pulverised salted fermented fish, most often anchovies. Has a pungent smell and strong taste; use sparingly.

five-spice powder a fragrant mixture of ground cinnamon, clove, star anise, sichuan pepper and fennel seeds.

flour (plain) an all-purpose flour, made from wheat.

french dressing a simple combination of oil and vinegar, usually seasoned with salt, pepper and various herbs.

fresh herbs we have specified when to use fresh or dried herbs. You can substitute 1 teaspoon dried herbs instead of 4 teaspoons (1 tablespoon) chopped fresh herbs.

garlic chives also known as chinese chives; have a wide, flat and hollow stem and posses a distinct garlic flavour.

gnocchi dumplings usually made of potato or semolina; can be boiled, baked or fried.

green peppercorns soft, unripe berry of the pepper plant usually sold packed in brine (occasionally found dried, packed in salt); a distinctive fresh taste.

harissa a spicy condiment made from chillies, garlic, coriander, cumin, caraway and olive oil.

hoisin sauce a thick, sweet and spicy Chinese paste made from salted fermented soy beans, onions and garlic.

instant noodles also known as 2 minute noodles; quick cooking noodles with a flavour sachet.

kalamata olives small brine-cured black olives.

kecap manis also known as ketjap manis; an Indonesian thick soy sauce with sugar and spices added.

kaffir lime leaves aromatic leaves of a small citrus tree bearing a wrinkled-skinned yellow-green fruit; used fresh or dried.

kumara Polynesian name of orange-fleshed sweet potato often confused with yam.

laksa paste bottled paste containing lemon grass, chillies, galangal, shrimp paste, onions and turmeric.

lavash bread flat, unleavened bread; also called lavoche.

lemon grass a tall, clumping, lemon-smelling and tasting, sharp-edged grass; the white lower part of each stem is chopped and used.

mesclun a mixture of baby lettuces and other salad leaves, also known as gourmet salad mix.

mince meat also known as ground meat.

mirin sweet rice wine used in Japanese cooking; sometimes referred to simply as rice wine but not to be confused with sake, rice wine made for drinking.

mushrooms

BUTTON small, cultivated white mushrooms having a delicate, subtle flavour.

FLAT large, soft, flat mushrooms with a rich earthy flavour; often misnamed field mushrooms.

OYSTER (abalone) grey-white mushroom shaped like a fan.

SHIITAKE also sold as donko mushrooms; available fresh and dried. Have a unique meaty flavour, which is stronger when dried.

SWISS BROWN also known as cremini or roman; light to dark brown mushrooms with full-bodied flavour. Button or cup mushrooms can be substituted.

mustard

DIJON a pale brown, distinctively flavoured, mild French mustard.

SEEDED also known as wholegrain. A French-style coarse-grain mustard made from crushed mustard seeds and dijon-style French mustard.

nachos topping sauce consists of pinto beans, tomato paste, onion, capsicum, jalpeños and garlic.

noodles

BEAN THREAD also called cellophane; made from green mung bean flour.

CRISPY FRIED sold packaged, usually a 100g packet, already deep-fried and ready to eat. Also known as crunchy noodles; available in two widths – thin and spaghetti-like or wide and flat like fettuccine.

FRESH EGG made from wheat flour and eggs; strands varying in thickness.

FRESH RICE thick, wide, almost white in colour; made from rice and vegetable oil. Must be covered with boiling water to remove starch and excess oil before use.

FRESH WHEAT commonly labelled hokkien mee or stir-fry noodles; round, thick, yellow-beige noodles.

HOKKIEN also known as stir-fry noodles; fresh wheat flour noodles resembling thick, yellow-brown spaghetti needing no pre-cooking before use.

INSTANT also known as 2-minute noodles; quick cooking noodles with a flavour sachet.

RICE STICK a dried noodle, available flat and wide or very thin; made from rice, flour and water.

RICE VERMICELLI also known as rice-flour noodles; made from ground rice. Sold dried and are best either deep-fried, soaked then stir-fried or used in soups.

singapore noodles a thinner version of the hokkien noodle,

also made from wheat flour and are yellow-brown in colour.

onion

GREEN also knows as scallions or (incorrectly) shallots; immature onions picked before the bulbs have formed, having long, bright-green edible stalks.

RED also known as spanish, red spanish or bermuda onion; sweet flavoured and purple-red in colour.

SPRING have crisp, narrow green-leafed tops and a fairly large white bulb.

onion powder made from ground dehydrated onions.

oregano an aromatic, spicy Mediterranean herb sold as fresh sprigs or chopped dried leaves.

oyster sauce made from oysters and their brine, cooked with salt and soy sauce, and thickened with starches.

palm sugar also known as jaggery, gula jawa and gula melaka; made from the coconut palm. Dark brown to black in colour and usually sold in rock-hard cakes. Dark brown sugar can be substituted.

pappadums sun-dried wafers made from a combination of lentil and rice flours, oil and spices.

paprika ground dried red capsicum (bell pepper), available sweet or hot.

parsley, flat-leaf also known as continental or italian parsley.

pawpaw also known as papaya or papaw; large pear-shaped red-orange tropical fruit. Sometimes used unripe (green) in cooking.

peanut oil pressed from ground peanuts; most commonly used oil in Asian cooking because of its high smoke point.

penne short, straight macaroni cut on the diagonal, either smooth or grooved.

pesto an Italian paste or thick uncooked sauce that come in a variety of different flavours such as basil and sun-dried tomato.

pide (turkish bread) comes in long (about 45cm) flat loaves as well as individual rounds; made from wheat flour and sprinkled with sesame or black onion seeds.

pine nuts also known as pignoli; not really nuts but small, cream-coloured kernels from the cones of several types of pine tree.

pitta also known as lebanese bread; also spelled pita, this wheat-flour pocket bread is sold in large, flat pieces that separate easily into two thin rounds. Also pocket pitta.

pizza base made from flour, yeast, oil, salt and water.

plum sauce a thick, sweet and sour dipping sauce made from plums, vinegar, sugar, chillies and spices.

potato

KIPFLER small and finger-shaped, with a nutty flavour; good baked.

TINY NEW also known as chats; harvested young and has a waxy, paper-thin skin.

prosciutto cured, air-dried (unsmoked), pressed ham; usually sold thinly sliced.

puff pastry (ready-rolled) packaged sheets of frozen puff pastry; made from wheat flour, vegetable margarine or butter, salt, food acid and water.

ranch dressing a creamy salad dressing that consists of oil, sugar, vinegar, egg yolk, garlic, and salt.

rice

BASMATI a white, fragrant long-grain rice; should be washed several times before cooking.

JASMINE fragrant long-grain rice; white rice can be substituted but will not taste the same.

WHITE LONG-GRAIN elongated grain, remains separate when cooked.

rocket also known as arugula, rugula and rucola; a peppery-tasting green leaf. Baby rocket is smaller and less peppery.

rosemary a strong, aromatic herb, used to season meat, poultry, and vegetables. Sold as fresh sprigs or dried leaves.

sage a grey-green leaf herb with a slightly bitter flavour and distinctive aroma. Sold as fresh sprigs or dried leaves.

salsa a combination of tomato, onion, pepper, vinegar, herbs and spices. Available in chunky-style and varying degrees of hotness.

sambal oelek (also ulek or olek) Indonesian in origin; a salty paste made from ground chillies.

satay sauce traditional Indonesian/Malaysian spicy peanut sauce.

sesame oil made from roasted, crushed white sesame seeds. Do not use for frying.

sesame seeds tiny oval seeds harvested from the tropical plant *sesamum indicum*.

snow peas also called *mange tout* ("eat all"). Snow pea sprouts produce succulent stems and leaves.

spinach also known as english spinach and incorrectly, silverbeet; has tender green leaves. Baby spinach leaves are slightly more tender.

sourdough rolls made from fermented flour, sugar, and water; has a distinctive sour or tangy taste.

soy sauce made from fermented soy beans. Light soy sauce is light in colour but generally quite salty. Salt-reduced soy sauce contains less salt.

sultanas golden raisins.

sugar snap peas small pods with small, formed peas inside; eaten whole, raw or cooked.

taco seasoning mix a packaged seasoning meant to duplicate the Mexican sauce made from oregano, cumin, chillies and other spices.

tamarind concentrate a thick, purple-black, ready-to-use paste extracted from the pulp of the tamarind bean.

tarragon a fragrant, distinctively sweet herb; sold as fresh sprigs or dried chopped leaves.

teriyaki sauce home made or commercially bottled; usually made from soy sauce, mirin, sugar, ginger and other spices.

thyme has a warm, herby taste and can be used fresh or dried.

tomato pasta sauce prepared sauce available from supermarkets.

tomato sauce also known as ketchup or catsup; a flavoured condiment made from slow-cooked tomatoes, vinegar and spices.

tortilla thin, round unleavened bread originating in Mexico. Available in wheat flour or corn varieties.

turmeric a member of the ginger family, the root is dried and ground, resulting in a rich yellow powder. It is intensely pungent in taste but not hot.

tzatziki a Greek yogurt and cucumber dish sometimes containing mint and/or garlic.

vegetable mix (frozen) consists of frozen corn, peas, capsicum, carrot and other vegetables.

vietnamese mint not a mint at all, this narrow-leafed, pungent herb, also known as cambodian mint and laksa leaf (daun laksa) is widely used in many Asian soups and salads.

vinegar

BALSAMIC authentic only from the province of Modena, Italy; made from a regional wine of white trebbiano grapes specially processed then aged in antique wooden casks to give an exquisite pungent flavour.

MALT made from fermented malted barley.

RED WINE based on fermented red wine.

RICE made from fermented rice, colourless and flavoured with sugar and salt. Also known as seasoned rice vinegar.

WHITE WINE made from white wine.

witlof also known as chicory or belgian endive.

worcestershire sauce a thin, dark-brown spicy sauce used as a seasoning and condiment.

yogurt we used unflavoured full-fat yogurt in our recipes unless stated otherwise.

zucchini also known as courgette.

index

almonds, chicken and..........7
angel hair pasta, chicken
  and rocket...................56
asparagus and potatoes
  in garlic cream
    sauce, chicken,...........46

baked pasta and
  chicken carbonara.........81
bok choy, spicy barbecued
  chicken and...............100
burger with the lot...........73
burgers, chicken schnitzel...39
burgers, mexican.............62

cacciatore-style sauce,
  chicken with...............89
caesar salad, chicken.........95
cajun chicken with
  creole rice.................42
cantonese stir-fry on
  noodle cakes.................8
capsicum, roasted, fetta
  and walnut salad...........80
carbonara, chicken,
  baked pasta and...........81
char-grilled chicken with
  warm tomato salad........54
chicken and almonds..........7
chicken and corn tartlets....45
chicken and couscous salad...6
chicken and crunchy
  noodle salad...............72
chicken and lime
  noodle salad...............92
chicken and mixed
  mushroom stir-fry..........10
chicken and vegie pie
  with fillo top...............86
chicken caesar salad..........95
chicken carbonara,
  baked pasta and...........81
chicken nachos..............111
chicken pho.................112
chicken ratatouille...........52
chicken salad, greek.........98
chicken salad, sesame.......110
chicken salad, tangy.........99
chicken salad, thai..........78
chicken salad,
  vietnamese.................94
chicken schnitzel burgers....39
chicken tenderloins in
  green peppercorn and
    tarragon dressing........60
chicken thighs,
  portuguese-style...........71
chicken tostadas.............82
chicken turnovers...........107
chicken with almonds
  and date sauce............102
chicken with
  cacciatore-style sauce.....89
chicken with creamy sun-
  dried tomato sauce......106
chicken with cucumber
  and tomato salsa...........63
chicken with olives
  and lemon.................103
chicken wraps................74
chicken, asparagus and
  potatoes in garlic
    cream sauce.............46

chicken, basil and
  cabbage salad..............90
chicken, cajun, with
  creole rice.................42
chicken, cashew and
  mesclun salad..............68
chicken, char-grilled, with
  warm tomato salad........54
chicken, creamy pesto,
  with gnocchi...............85
chicken, curried, and
  mushroom pies.............77
chicken, lemon basil,
  on hot potato salad.......69
chicken, lemon ginger.......76
chicken, mustard
  and rosemary..............64
chicken, oven-
  baked parmesan..........36
chicken, pide and
  haloumi salad................4
chicken, roast, with
  pea mash and gravy.......40
chicken, spicy barbecued,
  and bok choy.............100
chicken, sweet and sour.....58
chicken, thai, and rice.......65
chicken, thai, in
  lettuce-leaf cups.........104
chicken, thai,
  peanut-crusted.............43
chicken, witlof and
  cashew salad...............96
coriander and chilli
  grilled fillets...............66
corn tartlets,
  chicken and...............45
couscous salad,
  chicken and.................6
couscous, moroccan
  chicken salad with.........91
creamy pesto chicken
  with gnocchi...............85
creole rice, cajun
  chicken with...............42
crispy mustard tenderloins...38
cucumber and tomato
  salsa, chicken with........63
curried chicken and
  mushroom pies.............77

date sauce, chicken with
  almonds and..............102
drumettes, satay.............50
drumettes, tandoori, with
  cucumber raita.............44

fetta and walnut salad,
  roasted capsicum,.........80
fillets, coriander and
  chilli grilled................66

gnocchi, creamy pesto
  chicken with...............85
gravy, roast chicken with
  pea mash and..............40
greek chicken salad.........98
green peppercorn and
  tarragon dressing, chicken
    tenderloins in............60

haloumi salad, chicken,
  pide and.....................4

kebabs with pawpaw salsa...59

lemon basil chicken on hot
  potato salad...............69
lemon ginger chicken........76
lettuce-leaf cups,
  thai chicken in...........104

mexican burgers.............62
mexi-wings with
  cherry tomato salsa........49
moroccan chicken salad
  with couscous.............91
mushroom pies, curried
  chicken and...............77
mustard and
  rosemary chicken..........64

nachos, chicken.............111
noodle cakes, cantonese
  stir-fry on..................8
noodle salad, chicken
  and lime...................92
noodle, crunchy, salad,
  chicken and...............72

olives and lemon,
  chicken with..............103
oven-baked
  parmesan chicken..........36

pappadums, tandoori
  chicken salad with........70
parmesan chicken,
  oven-baked................36
pasta, angel hair,
  chicken and rocket........56
pasta, baked, and
  chicken carbonara........81
pawpaw salsa, kebabs with...59
pea mash and gravy, roast
  chicken with..............40
peanut-crusted thai chicken...43
pesto chicken salad..........55
pho, chicken................112
pide and haloumi
  salad, chicken..............4
pie, chicken and vegie,
  with fillo top..............86
pies, curried chicken
  and mushroom.............77
pizza, supreme..............48
portuguese-style
  chicken thighs............71
potatoes in garlic cream
  sauce, chicken,
    asparagus and...........46
pumpkin soup, thai-style....88

raita, cucumber, tandoori
  drumettes with...........44
ratatouille, chicken.........52
rice, thai chicken and......65
roast chicken with pea
  mash and gravy..........40
roasted capsicum, fetta
  and walnut salad..........80
rocket, angel hair pasta,
  chicken and...............56

salad, chicken and couscous...6
salad, chicken and
  crunchy noodle...........72

salad, chicken and
  lime noodle...............92
salad, chicken caesar.........95
salad, chicken, basil
  and cabbage..............90
salad, chicken, cashew
  and mesclun..............68
salad, chicken, pide
  and haloumi................4
salad, chicken, witlof
  and cashew...............96
salad, greek chicken.........98
salad, hot potato, lemon
  basil chicken on..........69
salad, moroccan chicken,
  with couscous.............91
salad, pesto chicken.........55
salad, roasted capsicum,
  fetta and walnut..........80
salad, sesame chicken.......110
salad, tandoori chicken,
  with pappadums...........70
salad, tangy chicken.........99
salad, thai chicken..........78
salad, vietnamese chicken...94
salad, warm tomato,
  char-grilled chicken with...54
salsa, cherry tomato,
  mexi-wings with...........49
salsa, cucumber and
  tomato, chicken with.....63
satay drumettes.............50
sauce, cacciatore-style,
  chicken with...............89
sauce, creamy sun-dried
  tomato, chicken with....106
sauce, date, chicken with
  almonds and..............102
schnitzel, chicken, burgers...39
sesame chicken salad.......110
soup, thai-style pumpkin....88
spicy barbecued chicken
  and bok choy.............100
sticky barbecue wings.......51
sun-dried tomato sauce,
  creamy, chicken with....106
supreme pizza...............48
sweet and sour chicken......58

tandoori chicken salad
  with pappadums...........70
tandoori drumettes with
  cucumber raita...........44
tangy chicken salad.........99
tartlets, chicken and corn...45
tenderloins, chicken, in
  green peppercorn and
    tarragon dressing........60
tenderloins, crispy mustard...38
thai chicken and rice........65
thai chicken in
  lettuce-leaf cups..........104
thai chicken salad...........78
thai-style pumpkin soup.....88
tom kha gai................108
tostadas, chicken...........82

vegie pie, chicken and,
  with fillo top..............86
vietnamese chicken salad...94

wings, sticky barbecue.......51
wraps, chicken..............74

facts and figures

Wherever you live, you'll be able to use our recipes with the help of these easy-to-follow conversions. While these conversions are approximate only, the difference between an exact and the approximate conversion of various liquid and dry measures is but minimal and will not affect your cooking results.

dry measures

metric	imperial
15g	1/2oz
30g	1oz
60g	2oz
90g	3oz
125g	4oz (1/4lb)
155g	5oz
185g	6oz
220g	7oz
250g	8oz (1/2lb)
280g	9oz
315g	10oz
345g	11oz
375g	12oz (3/4lb)
410g	13oz
440g	14oz
470g	15oz
500g	16oz (1lb)
750g	24oz (11/2lb)
1kg	32oz (2lb)

oven temperatures

These oven temperatures are only a guide. Always check the manufacturer's manual.

	°C (Celsius)	°F (Fahrenheit)	Gas Mark
Very slow	120	250	1
Slow	150	300	2
Moderately slow	160	325	3
Moderate	180 - 190	350 - 375	4
Moderately hot	200 - 210	400 - 425	5
Hot	220 - 230	450 - 475	6
Very hot	240 - 250	500 - 525	7

liquid measures

metric	imperial
30ml	1 fluid oz
60ml	2 fluid oz
100ml	3 fluid oz
125ml	4 fluid oz
150ml	5 fluid oz (1/4 pint/1 gill)
190ml	6 fluid oz
250ml	8 fluid oz
300ml	10 fluid oz (1/2 pint)
500ml	16 fluid oz
600ml	20 fluid oz (1 pint)
1000ml (1 litre)	13/4 pints

helpful measures

metric	imperial
3mm	1/8in
6mm	1/4in
1cm	1/2in
2cm	3/4in
2.5cm	1in
5cm	2in
6cm	21/2in
8cm	3in
10cm	4in
13cm	5in
15cm	6in
18cm	7in
20cm	8in
23cm	9in
25cm	10in
28cm	11in
30cm	12in (1ft)

helpful measures

The difference between one country's measuring cups and another's is, at most, within a 2 or 3 teaspoon variance. (For the record, 1 Australian metric measuring cup holds approximately 250ml.) The most accurate way of measuring dry ingredients is to weigh them. When measuring liquids, use a clear glass or plastic jug with the metric markings. (One Australian metric tablespoon holds 20ml; one Australian metric teaspoon holds 5ml.)

If you would like to purchase *The Australian Women's Weekly* Test Kitchen's metric measuring cups and spoons (as approved by Standards Australia), turn to page 120 for details and order coupon. You will receive:

- a graduated set of 4 cups for measuring dry ingredients, with sizes marked on the cups.
- a graduated set of 4 spoons for measuring dry and liquid ingredients, with amounts marked on the spoons.

Note: North America, NZ and the UK use 15ml tablespoons. All cup and spoon measurements are level.

We use large eggs having an average weight of 60g.

how to measure

When using graduated metric measuring cups, shake dry ingredients loosely into the appropriate cup. Do not tap the cup on a bench or tightly pack the ingredients unless directed to do so. Level top of measuring cups and measuring spoons with a knife. When measuring liquids, place a clear glass or plastic jug with metric markings on a flat surface to check accuracy at eye level.

Looking after **your interest...**

Keep your ACP cookbooks clean, tidy and within easy reach with slipcovers designed to hold up to 12 books. *Plus* you can follow our recipes perfectly with a set of accurate measuring cups and spoons, as used by *The Australian Women's Weekly* Test Kitchen.

To order

Mail or fax Photocopy and complete the coupon below and post to ACP Books Reader Offer, ACP Publishing, GPO Box 4967, Sydney NSW 2001, or fax to (02) 9267 4967.

Phone Have your credit card details ready, then phone 136 116 (Mon-Fri, 8.00am-6.00pm; Sat, 8.00am-6.00pm).

Price

Book Holder
Australia: $13.10 (incl. GST).
Elsewhere: $A21.95.

Metric Measuring Set
Australia: $6.50 (incl. GST).
New Zealand: $A8.00.
Elsewhere: $A9.95.
Prices include postage and handling.
This offer is available in all countries.

Payment

Australian residents We accept the credit cards listed on the coupon, money orders and cheques.

Overseas residents We accept the credit cards listed on the coupon, drafts in $A drawn on an Australian bank, and also British, New Zealand and U.S. cheques in the currency of the country of issue. Credit card charges are at the exchange rate current at the time of payment.

Photocopy and complete the coupon below

☐ **Book Holder**

☐ **Metric Measuring Set**
Please indicate number(s) required.

Mr/Mrs/Ms_____

Address_____

_____

Postcode _____ Country _____

Ph: Bus. Hours:( )_____

I enclose my cheque/money order for $ _____
payable to ACP Publishing

OR: please charge my

☐ Bankcard   ☐ Visa   ☐ MasterCard

☐ Diners Club   ☐ Amex

Card number

Expiry date ____/____

Cardholder's signature _____

Please allow up to 30 days for delivery within Australia.
Allow up to 6 weeks for overseas deliveries.
Both offers expire 31/12/02. HLCMIM02

Designer *Mary Keep*
Editor *Deborah Quick*
Test Kitchen Staff
Food director *Pamela Clark*
Food editor *Karen Hammial*
Assistant food editor *Amira Ibram*
Test kitchen manager *Elizabeth Hooper*
Senior home economist *Kimberley Cover*
Home economists *Emma Braz,
Naomi Scesny, Kelly Cruickshanks,
Sarah Hine, Sarah Hobbs, Alison Webb*
Editorial coordinator *Amanda Josling*
In-house stylist *Sarah Hobbs*
In-house photographer *Robert Taylor*
ACP Books Staff
Editorial director *Susan Tomnay*
Creative director *Hieu Nguyen*
Senior editors *Julie Collard, Liz Neate*
Editor *Deborah Quick*
Designers *Mary Keep, Caryl Wiggins,
Alison Windmill*
Studio manager *Caryl Wiggins*
Editorial coordinator *Holly van Oyen*
Editorial assistant *Georgie McShane*
Publishing manager (sales) *Jennifer McD*
Publishing manager (rights & new project
Jane Hazell
Production manager *Carol Currie*
Business manager *Sally Lees*
Chief executive officer *John Alexander*
Group publisher *Jill Baker*
Publisher *Sue Wannan*

Produced by ACP Books, Sydney.
Colour separations by ACP Colour
Graphics Pty Ltd, Sydney.
Printed by Dai Nippon Printing in Korea.
Published by ACP Publishing Pty Limited,
54 Park St, Sydney; GPO Box 4088,
Sydney, NSW 1028.
Ph: (02) 9282 8618 Fax: (02) 9267 9438.
acpbooks@acp.com.au
www.acpbooks.com.au
To order books, phone 136 116.
Send recipe enquiries to
recipeenquiries@acp.com.au
AUSTRALIA: Distributed by Network Serv
GPO Box 4088, Sydney, NSW 1028.
Ph: (02) 9282 8777
Fax: (02) 9264 3278.
UNITED KINGDOM: Distributed by Austra
Consolidated Press (UK), Moulton Park
Business Centre, Red House Rd, Moulton
Northampton, NN3 6AQ Ph: (01604) 497
Fax: (01604) 497 533 acpukltd@aol.com
CANADA: Distributed by Whitecap Books
351 Lynn Ave, North Vancouver, BC, V7J 2
Ph: (604) 980 9852.
NEW ZEALAND: Distributed by Netlink
Distribution Company, Level 4, 23 Hargrea
College Hill, Auckland 1, Ph: (9) 302 7616
SOUTH AFRICA: Distributed by PSD Prom
(Pty) Ltd, PO Box 1175, Isando 1600, SA,
Ph: (011) 392 6065.

Chicken meals in minutes
Includes index.
ISBN 1 86396 260 3
1. Cookery (Poultry). 2. Quick and easy
cookery. I. Title: Australian Women's Wee
(Series: Australian Women's Weekly).
641.665
© ACP Publishing Pty Limited 2002
ABN 18 053 273 546
This publication is copyright. No part of it
be reproduced or transmitted in any form
without the written permission of the publi
First published 2002.